RAVE REVIEW

"This is a fun, fascinating and thought prov
realms of personal development, self coaching an
stories, models and exercises that can enrich and enhance the life of every single
person." - Natalie Heeley, Global Business Coach

"Nothing less than sensational. Full of captivating stories that teach as they
delight. This book will change your life." - Michaela Quilici, Coach

"An elegant self coaching model and powerful formula for true success
and happiness. I really enjoyed the stories and seeing how these tools helped
people develop more successful lives. I especially loved the concept of how to fail
successfully." - Deb Connors, Speaker & Consultant

"Full of wonderful stories, practical tools and a self coaching model that
can transform your life." - Derek LaCroix, Counsellor

"This is a masterful use of stories on how to shift your own inner
limitations. I've always believed that stories are a vital contributor to high
performance on all fronts, and so it's great to see it all laid out here. I couldn't
put this book down"
- Mary Sue Rabe, Coach, Speaker and Author

"A wonderfully crafted book revealing a simple but powerful model
for managing your mind that can improve the quality of anyone's life. I'm
recommending this game changing book to all of my clients."
- Jerry Conti, Entrepreneur

"Carla and Dave have taken a complex subject and made it accessible to
anyone who reads it. Through fascinating stories they show how to transform
the negativity that repeatedly blocks a person's progress towards success."
- Kamile Kapel, Vancouver filmmaker & videographer

MindStory
Inner Coach

Overcome Your Past Stories so You Can
Build Your Business, Make a Bigger
Difference AND Make a Great Living

DAVE O'CONNOR & CARLA RIEGER

Legal Disclaimer

No part of this material may be used, reproduced, distributed or transmitted in any form and by any means whatsoever, including without limitation, by photocopying, recording or other electronic or mechanical methods or by any information storage and retrieval system without the prior written permission from the author, except for brief excerpts in a review.

This book is intended to provide general information only. Neither the author nor the publisher provides any legal or other professional advice. If you need professional advice, you should seek advice from the appropriate licensed professional. This book does not provide complete information on the subject matter covered. This book is not intended to address specific requirements, either for an individual or an organization. This book is intended to be used only as a general guide and not as a sole source of information on the subject matter. While the author has undertaken diligent efforts to ensure accuracy, there is no guarantee of accuracy or of no errors, omissions or typographical errors. Any slights of people or organizations are unintentional. The author and publisher shall have no liability or responsibility to any person or entity and hereby disclaim all liability, including without limitation, liability for consequential damages regarding any claim, loss or damage that may be incurred, or alleged to have been incurred, directly or indirectly, arising out of the information provided in this book.

ISBN # 9781086051216

Copyright © 2019 by Carla Rieger & Dave O'Connor
Edited by Tania Cogan and Beth Bruno
All rights reserved. No part of this publication may be reproduced or
transmitted in any form or by any means, electronic, or mechanical, including
photocopying, recording, or by any information storage and retrieval system.

Visit us on the web: www.MindStoryAcademy.com
E-Mail: Carla@MindStoryAcademy.com or Dave@MindStoryAcademy.com
Facebook: https://www.facebook.com/MindStoryAcademy/

The Artistry of Change Productions Inc.
https://.ArtistryofChange.com

DEDICATION

We dedicate this book to all our clients and teachers
over the years who taught us about how to free
our minds and live with passion and purpose.

Table of Contents

INTRODUCTION

SECTION 1 – ACCEPTANCE

SECTION 2 – VISION

SECTION 3 – ACTION

SECTION 4 – REPROGRAM

SECTION 5 – ATTENTION

CONCLUSION

INTRODUCTION

How to Get the Best Results from this Book

Do you ever feel like there's something holding you back? Maybe you sense that you could be living a life that's more free, expressive, prosperous and on purpose. If so, then this book is for you.

Maybe your belief levels are up and down and sometimes self-doubt wins out. That happens to most of us. Perhaps you're procrastinating? You want to take more of the actions that you KNOW you should be taking, and you're frustrated at your slow progress.

If so, it might be a sign you're sabotaging your own success and don't even realize it.

Your results are up to you, but the main purpose for this book is to get you some immediate results in your business and life. And, in the interest of full disclosure, we're hoping that you get such great value from our MindStory Inner Coaching and AVARA Model, that when you next think of investing in your personal and business development, whether it's now or later, that you will consider working with us at **https://MindStoryAcademy.com/**.

Maybe your confidence levels go up and down but sometimes self-doubt wins out

It's been proven that successful people maintain a positive focus in life, no matter what is going on around them. At the same time, they also are aware of the harsh realities of life and take the necessary steps to deal with them, as best as possible. They stay focused on their important goals despite it all.

While that is the ideal, it can be difficult to maintain a positive focus and not let distractions and obstacles win. Maybe you try to stay focused on the vision of who you want to become. Then, in the early hours of the morning, you catch yourself brooding over a past failure, an embarrassing mistake, or a lost opportunity. This darkens the rest of your day. You lose your positive focus and get lost in a low vibrational state of mind.

You're not alone. This world seems designed to keep us stuck in negativity, distractions and self-sabotage so that we don't realize our fullest potential. One perspective on this situation is the possibility that life is a just game, or a school you attend to learn important skills. Once you learn them, you can rise to the next level of evolution. If so, then all this negativity and sabotage can be seen as a gift; as a game handicap. If it were all so easy, you wouldn't learn anything.

The good news is that you can break free from that mind enslavement game of the world, and set your own course in life, be your own authority and live the life you were meant to live, and therefore learn and grow.

The methods in this book will help you do a regular "mind reset" so you can refocus and take inspired action, whenever you need to. ***The trick is to practice this over and over again*** until it becomes your default pattern, until it overrides the bad habits of mind you learned as a child. Many of those bad habits then got reinforced throughout your life; that's why repetition is important to transforming them.

Use these methods over and over again whenever you feel stuck. After awhile, you won't even need the processes. You'll be able to do a mind reset quickly and naturally. These are like training wheels on your bike, until you get the hang of doing it yourself.

Now, I know you didn't pay much for this book, but please listen very carefully. The worst mistake you can make is to treat this like it has little value, which means to put it on the back burner and never do anything with it. This MindStory Inner Coaching can change your life profoundly... it can be worth tens of thousands or more in additional income for you, and it can mean the difference between consistently waking up excited about the day or dreading it.

So, we invite you to act as if you just paid AT LEAST $500 for this book. Take 30 minutes that you might normally spend scrolling through Facebook, watching a TV show, or getting lost in the YouTube vortex... and invest that time in upgrading your mind. Pay attention as intently as you've ever read anything before.

This CAN be the turning point for you in your quest to become more successful in the areas of your life where you feel like you're spinning your wheels, so that you can finally feel like you're living that which you've only been dreaming about up until now.

These dreams for our future - we believe these are messages from your "future ideal self," telling you the right direction to go; giving you breadcrumbs along the way if you listen and pay attention. The problem is that most people don't listen deeply. They allow the fears and distractions to keep them off the path that would most lead to a life of satisfaction. Allow this MindStory Inner Coaching to bring you to your future ideal self.

What is a Mindstory?

A MindStory is what you tell yourself about life at the subconscious level, below your awareness. They are stories from the past, present and imaginings about the future. Some of these MindStories are empowering and supportive of the life you were meant to live, while others are disempowering and sabotage your life.

For example, I once coached two women. They were sisters. I worked with them both for 5 years when they were in their forties. They had a similar upbringing and looked similar. That said, Kate had a hard time keeping a job, but a loving and supportive husband. She was overweight with a bad back, yet was generally happy and spent a lot of time doing creative projects.

On the other hand, Andrea was the head of her own successful company, but had a husband who cheated on her several times. She was thin, physically healthy and stayed in shape but was usually feeling unhappy and frustrated by life.

The difference? They had totally different MindStories.

MindStories include many areas of life such as:

- how worthy you are of good things
- what you can or can't accomplish
- how people should relate to you
- how happy you can be
- how supported you are by life

- how healthy your body can be
- how much money you can make
- and much more

Transforming those stories changes your life for the better in the quickest, most profound ways you could ever imagine. Most people don't bother to learn this massively useful skill and go on to live lives of quiet desperation. It really is such a shame, when there are so many tools now, like the ones here, to help people break free and re-write their own MindStories.

According to neuroscience, we remember bad experiences far more than positive ones. At the same time, for every challenging thing in your life, chances are hundreds of things went well. We just forget all that. The primitive brain imprints negative memories to ensure your survival. For example, if you burn your hand, the subconscious mind will imprint that into your long-term memory so you won't do it again. It won't imprint a beautiful sunset because that's not important to your survival.

The downside is that all those bad experiences are at the forefront of your memory banks, the ones that are easy to access. Those memories influence decisions moving forward. For example, a client, Linda, was humiliated in school by her teacher, who showed her failing grade on a math test to the whole class. This made her avoid all classes that involved math after that. She spent years exploring careers that weren't right for her. Then, she learned how to change her MindStory on math. Now, she is the Chief Financial Officer of a start-up health tech company that just received a huge round of funding, and she loves it.

The brain actually structures the programs in our subconscious mind in story form. To change them you need to understand the *limiting* story and rewrite the more *empowering* one by breaking both down first into their component parts. For example, a writer must get clear on characters, scripts, emotions, setting, plot, theme and conflict to create a compelling novel. This book will help you do that with your inner stories.

Most people need to be more professional at running their own mind. You're expected to be professional at running your business or career, and not treat it like a hobby. The vast majority of people are amateurs at running their minds and pay a big price without even realizing it.

It has become our life's mission at https://MindStoryAcademy.com/ to create a teachable system so that you can do it, too. In our experience of coaching people for decades, up to 90% of what made the biggest difference were the mindset tools we gave people. The truth is, you can have all the strategies in the world for business success, but if your mind is full of doubt, confusion or fear then you'll underperform and never achieve your dreams.

In this book we are teaching you how to be a good Inner Coach to yourself. At the Academy you can also take it a step further via our https://MindStoryAcademy.com/Certification.

Why this Book was Created

This book was created because we were able to overcome many huge challenges that we see others struggle with, and they asked us for help. We were able to help them, profoundly. As such we created a structure of what we had achieved in a way that people could really "get it" and "apply it".

Two people wrote this book, Dave O'Connor and Carla Rieger, because we believe that two heads are better than one. Many books on the market are written by either a man or a woman, but this one was written by both. At the core of every creative act, we believe there is a male aspect of the self and a female aspect of the self, combining to create a third entity – the creative fruit of that interaction.

That's why you'll see "Carla's Story" meaning, Carla Rieger's journey and perspective, and "Dave's Story" meaning, Dave O'Connor's journey and perspective. You may relate to one, the other, both or neither.

At the end of each chapter are 'HOMEPLAYS' which represent a combination of the two approaches in experiential form. They're designed to turn the ideas of this book into real world results for you.

The AVARA Self-Coaching Model

For many years, both of us were very successful in our own speaking and performance coaching business. Eventually we decided to combine our approaches, putting them into a repeatable system. That's when the magic happened at a whole other level. And thus the **AVARA Model** was born. That's why the book is structured using the five parts of the model. It makes breaking free of limiting mindsets quick and easy.

This book will explore the core model. If you want regular, personalized support with this model and dozens of our other tools, check out our monthly group coaching program called The MindStory Inner Circle, or MIC for short. Alternatively you can also explore private coaching at https://MindstoryAcademy.com/

In the meantime, try this self-coaching model on yourself to see how it works for you. Start by writing out the ISSUE. Getting issues down on paper, is the first step of transformation because you're becoming conscious of what we call "The Limiting MindStory".

Then, see if you can just state the FACTS without the emotions and interpretations. From an outside perspective what would everyone agree on. E.g. *My business partner is difficult to work with* is NOT a fact, it's an interpretation. *My business partner and I were discussing the product launch*, is a fact. This is an important skill to build, because most people confuse the two. They think their interpretations are facts. Only when you can see the difference will you be able to make a breakthrough. This process below can help you do that.

Step A – Issue: What's a problem in your life? Describe the situation. No editing. We'll refer to this as your Limiting MindStory.

E.g. My husband and I run a business together. I always thought of myself as a good communicator until we started the business. My husband often speaks to me in a harsh way, and I find myself getting reactive to him. I end up feeling disrespected and invalidated all the time. We are fighting over the smallest of things in the business.

Step B - Facts: Now see if you can state what you wrote above as objectively as possible. That means to separate facts from your interpretation, no adjectives, adverbs, descriptive phrases, or feelings. From an outside perspective what would everyone agree on?

E.g. Communicating about the business with my husband.

Step C – Limiting Story	Step D – Empowering Story
Now, you're going to break your MindStory down into its components parts here in the "Limiting Story" section. Then, we'll transform it in the "Empowering Story" section in the right-hand column. Start by going down this left column first, then go onto Step D, in the right-hand column.	Now that you've broken your MindStory down into its components parts, we'll transform it in this "Empowering Story". Look at what you wrote in each of the parts in the left column, and create a positive version here.
1) Acceptance: What are the limiting feelings, thoughts and meaning you are giving to the situation? Express it like this: *I am* (negative feeling) *because* (negative thought). *I'm making this situation mean…* (your interpretation).	**1) Acceptance**: What are more empowering feelings, thoughts and meanings you could give to the situation? Express it like this *I have chosen to be* (positive feeling) *because* (positive thought). *A better meaning I could give this situation is…*
*E.g. **I'm feeling** judgmental of myself and him **because** we are fighting so much. **I'm making this mean** that he doesn't care about me.*	*E.g. **I have chosen to feel** compassionate towards myself and him, **because** we are going through a challenging time. **A better meaning is** that this might be a gift, reminding us to get back to good communication habits.*

I AM FEELING	*I HAVE CHOSEN TO BE*
_____	_____
_____	_____
_____	_____
BECAUSE	*BECAUSE*
_____	_____
_____	_____
_____	_____
I'M MAKING THIS MEAN (list all, even if they seem unlikely or silly)	*A BETTER MEANING (an interpretation that would empower)*
_____	_____
_____	_____
_____	_____
2) Vision: What is your possible future A YEAR FROM NOW if you live from this limiting MindStory? Be specific. *E.g. Unhappy marriage, separation or divorce.*	**2) Vision:** What is your possible future A YEAR FROM NOW if you live from this more empowering MindStory? Be specific. *E.g. We have found our way back to being loving, compassionate and respectful towards each other. The business is enjoyable and thriving.*

3) **Action:** What action or inaction is taking place? *E.g. We are constantly fighting*	3) **Action:** What actions could you take to achieve this empowering VISION? Anything goes. No editing. List at least 7 ideas. Then choose 1 idea and break it down to specific, small next steps in Step E below. *E.g. Take a time out if we get reactive* *1.* *2.* *3.* *4.* *5.* *6.* *7.*
4) **Reprogram:** What is a recent event or experience that triggered this issue? Use present tense as if you were there now. *E.g. I've just reorganized the kitchen. My husband is looking for our large salad bowl and can't find it. He says in a harsh tone of voice "Where is the salad bowl?!!" Then, I shout back at him, "How dare you talk to me like that!! It's so disrespectful and unkind." And then it escalates further. We finally stop and eat our dinner, in silence, in different parts of the house.*	4) **Reprogram:** What is a similar event or experience that might happen in the near future where it's playing out in a more empowering way? Use present tense as if you were there now. *E.g. My husband is getting triggered, and I respond in a skillful way. I express understanding and compassion for where he's coming from. I'm using good communication skills. I'm tapped into my life purpose as a teacher of good communication skills, and so I'm seeing this situation as a chance to become even more skilled.*

5) **Attention**: What are the limiting beliefs here or negative Self Talk? List all even if they seem mean-spirited, unlikely or silly. *E.g. I'm a bad communicator. He's a jerk.*	5) **Attention**: What might be your new beliefs or Self Talk from this more empowering MindStory? Start your sentence with this progressive affirmation: "Every day in every way I'm …" *E.g. Every day in every way I'm more easily switching out of a triggered state and taking care of myself and my husband.*

Step E - Specific Next Actions: Pick one idea from your empowering ACTION section above. What are 1 to 3 specific, small, next steps to get that started? Give each a date, delegate where possible. By breaking down big goals into small steps, it makes them feel easier to accomplish.

#	Action	Who	When
Eg	*Invite John to sit down with me to revisit the good communication habits we used to have, and see which ones we both want to commit to using.*	John & I	Tuesday
1.			
2.			
3.			

The AVARA model can break people free of anything, anytime, anywhere. We wanted to let you know where this came from, because once you apply it regularly life tends to change dramatically for the better.

Both of us are creative types, maybe like you. We love strategy, but at the core of who we are the inner creative genius is what we like to cultivate in ourselves and others. Much of what we're taught in school devalues our human creative spirit. Yet you NEED that to be a leader and business owner who makes a difference for others. To truly provide value in the world these days you need to help people break out of the norms so they can be successful on their own terms, as opposed to a slave to past conditioning.

That's probably what attracted you to having a business in the first place – the creative freedom of it all, right? All acts of creativity have the same basic structure. A feminine aspect comes together with a masculine aspect to create the third and new possibility. You can see this in the Taoist principles of Yin and Yang, the Hindu principles of Shiva and Shakti. You can see these principles in all the major religious and spiritual traditions. You also see it in the basic mechanics of electricity. In fact, we live in a binary world, where the interaction of the polarities is what creates new possibilities.

This became more obvious when we came together as a couple, seeing how the integration of the masculine and feminine principles creates both the inner and outer transformation. For example, transforming your belief in yourself leads to more confidence while making your offerings to the world, which leads to more income and more people being served. It works in the opposite direction as well. Feeding your disbelief in yourself then leads to less confidence while making your offerings to the world, which leads to less income and fewer people being served.

The AVARA Model

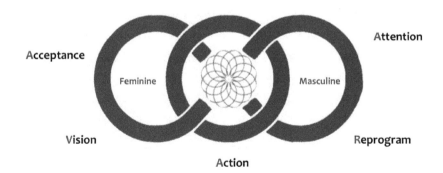

The model has 5 parts, starting in the realm of the feminine principle and crossing over into the masculine as you can see in the image – ending in transformation in the middle. Many coaching models are either too masculine or too feminine. The masculine model tends to be all action, analysis, focus. That structure creates results but often at the cost of the deeper part of the self...where the ends justify the means. For example, making money for money's sake, or being busy for busyness sake. Not connected to a source of wisdom or true life's purpose.

Alternatively, you can find models that are all about diving deep into the feminine, into the source energy of wisdom, deep intuition, right brain artistry, but with little connection to left brain analysis, action and focus. It's where you can get lost in the world of ungrounded dreams.

Any model of transformation needs to have both principles in order for real, long lasting transformation to occur. That's why we created the model as we did.

Most of us start out in life with limiting MindStories. These are thoughts, beliefs, feelings, perspectives picked up when our brains are wide open and we absorb learning like a sponge. Some of those learnings are useful, empowering and lead to a fulfilling life, while others create blockages, disempowerment and lead to an unfulfilling life. It's useful to explore what are the limiting MindStories you picked up, and how to use the model to transform them. Here are two examples.

CARLA'S LIMITING MINDSTORY

I grew up in a home where being goal-oriented, proper and serious were important. My parents loved me, but fun, playfulness and noise were not tolerated. Fast forward to age 23 and I am a very serious person, too. I am working three part-time jobs and taking a full load of university courses. I am going to be a lawyer or journalist or business leader. Something important. Something ambitious.

The problem is, I am barely passing my courses. I'd been labelled dyslexic as a child. It takes me forever to read the long textbooks. I'm procrastinating with my assignments and pulling all-nighters to get them done. I'm overweight and hooked on caffeine, alcohol and cigarettes to get through the days and nights. I have a skin allergy, chronic digestive issues, no social life, and low level depression.

One day I decide to try a public speaking course. I'm the youngest person in the program, but I figure this will help me get past my shyness. The teacher, along with sixty other students, sits in the audience. It's my turn on stage. With a furrowed brow, I begin reading from my notes. The room fills with sounds of the shaking paper in my hands.

Three minutes into my speech, the teacher shouts out in a Bronx accent, "Honey, stop right there!"

I look up. Terrified. "What?"

"How old are you?"

"I'm 23, why?"

"Because you act like a 45-year-old insurance underwriter."

The room breaks into laughter. My brow furrows even more. I think... anything to do with insurance can't be good. What she says next really rattles me.

"You're so serious. You're young. Try having more fun when you speak. If you're this serious now, what are you going to be like in 20 years? Lighten up already. Go lighten up and then you can come back to my course. Get off the stage."

She gave me some ideas about how to go lighten up. I remember driving home that day thinking – maybe she's right. It was a turning point in my life. It caused me to take a good, hard look at my life and where I was headed. All I did was work. My wardrobe consisted of colors such as grey, dark grey, and off grey. Photos of fun social events showed everyone smiling, except for me. Something had to change.

I dropped everything and made a complete right turn in my life—and did something very weird, which my parents did NOT approve of!

It marked the beginning of breaking me free from the beliefs and bad habits that kept me locked up. It was the beginning of my first big MindStory shift. I've now spent decades dedicated to learning and teaching people how to free their minds to have a more fulfilling personal and professional life.

I'll tell you how that happened a bit later…

DAVE'S LIMITING MINDSTORY

I remember this particular day I went to the ATM. I put my card in and all it said was "insufficient funds". That was the rock bottom of a slippery downward slope I'd been on for a long time.

I was a struggling salesman, seriously lacking in confidence and belief in myself. I lacked direction. In fact, for 2 years I held the record for consistently losing the most money within my company. The running joke at the monthly sales meetings was, "I wonder who's at the bottom of the leaderboard this month? Oh look, it's Dave, again!" Every day I went to work feeling like I was a fraud. I was miserable.

Before I started the job, I had taken out a loan of £1500 for a car that was now falling apart. The intention was to pay off the loan quickly as soon as I was making money. What an illusion that turned out to be! I got seriously in debt. Not only could I not pay back the loan, I couldn't afford to pay for car insurance or repairs. I kept ignoring the ever-increasing warning lights that were showing up on my dashboard. Every day I got into the car praying that it wouldn't fall completely apart and that I'd make it safely to work.

Then, one day, I was driving like a maniac, late for work again. I was speeding towards one of Dublin's busiest roundabouts and hit the brakes to slow down, but the car did not slow down. The brakes had failed. I was driving full speed into the roundabout with cars coming into it from all directions!

I'll get back to what happened a bit later…

That moment was the beginning of my first big MindStory shift.

Where to Start

In our experience of coaching people for over 40 years combined, most issues can be tracked back to one of five symptoms. It's some version of fear, doubt, procrastination, confusion or distraction.

As such, the AVARA model is designed to cover all those bases. Therefore, you don't necessarily need to start the model at the beginning. Based on your particular issue, it may make sense to start filling out a different part of the model first. Here's a table that can be a helpful guide.

YOUR SYMPTOM	YOUR SELF TALK	WHERE TO START IN THE AVARA MODEL	SECTION
Fear	*Something is blocking me and I'm not sure what it is*	**Acceptance**	1
Confusion	*I am overwhelmed and working really hard but still don't seem to be getting anywhere*	**Vision**	2
Procrastination	*I can't seem to get myself to take the important actions I know I need to take*	**Action**	3
Doubt	*I have this vision/goal for my life, but I just don't believe it's possible*	**Reprogram**	4
Distraction	*I start every day with good intentions, but find myself easily going off track*	**Attention**	5

For example, a client named Rachel was laid off from her job. As part of a severance package, she was sent to a career guidance center. After testing, they labelled her as ADHD (Attention Deficit Hyperactivity Disorder). Her dream was to move out of assistant type roles and into leadership roles, but the tests suggested this wouldn't be a good path for her, given the ADHD. We started her coaching series focused on distraction versus attention, which is part 5 of the model.

Here we focus on building the strength of the focus dimension of the brain. It's the ability to zoom in on the details and also to zoom out on the big picture. It's also the ability to choose a focus for a task and stay there until completion. Digital media has impaired many people's ability to have a well-balanced focus dimension. Yet with the help of the AVARA Model, Rachel was able to rebuild her focus dimension and build her dream career.

Super Achiever Self-Assessment

Before we get into the book, try this quick self-assessment. One of the best ways to get results from this book is by first recognizing the areas where you need help. That way, you know where to focus.

If you are reading this book electronically, have a notebook nearby to record your answers. If you have a paper copy, you can just write in the space provided, or if you aren't one to mark-up books, you can write in a notebook as well.

So, are you ready? Here are the seven questions that are going to start the process of changing your life forever.

1. On a scale of 1 to 5, what has been your general level of ACCEPTANCE, compassion and curiosity for what's really going on with issues regarding your business/work life? _____

- A "5" is full compassion and curiosity. That's where you're saying, "I have issues, and it's okay. I'm willing to face them, discover what's really going, learn from them and turn them around.
- A "4" is where you usually have compassion for yourself, curiosity and willingness to learn so you can turn them around, but occasionally you avoid facing and dealing with issues. You catch yourself trying to distract or avoid.
- A "3" is where you've been going back and forth between judging yourself, having negative thoughts, feeling bad, blaming someone

or something else, and then being compassionate, curious and willing to accept and learn.

- A "2" is where you're in the negativity most of the time, and haven't been accepting, curious or compassionate with yourself. Maybe you have the odd thought about how this might be a counterproductive way to think, but you don't know how to break free.
- A "1" is rock bottom. You're feeling negative most of the time. You have no curiosity about how to transform this situation from the inside out.

2. On a scale of 1 to 5 how much are you on fire with a VISION for your business? _____

- A "5" is you're on fire with a burning desire. You're an unstoppable force with an invincible vision and your life reflects this.
- A "4" means you're above average. You're steadily growing yourself and your business every day and your life reflects this.
- A "3" means you're up and down. Your vision comes and goes, as does your motivation. Results are mediocre.
- A "2" means you're below average. You can't seem to find your vision. You may have had it before, but it's gone now. You can't seem to reconnect with a new goal. You're just going through the motions.
- A "1" means you're feeling totally lost and unclear. You just don't believe in yourself or in any vision.

3. On a scale of 1 to 5, what level of ACTION do you consistently take every day towards this vision? _____

The answer will determine how clear and exciting your vision is. If it's big, bold, and bright, and stands out in your mind, then you will be taking all the actions of a successful person.

- A "5" is world class. That's where you're saying, "I'm unstoppable right now." You take massive action every day in the direction of your big vision. As such, your life and business are growing exponentially.
- A "4" is excellent. You're definitely taking some consistent action, and the results in your business and life are steadily growing.
- A "3" is average. A lot of people are stuck here. You're doing the bare minimum to stay in the game.
- A "2" is below average. You're taking very little action. Hit and miss. Maybe every so often you take some action.
- A "1" is rock bottom; You're saying, "Help, I'm stuck. I just can't seem to get out of this rut."

4. On a scale of 1 to 5 rate your ability to REPROGRAM your thinking in the face of challenges so you can better reach your goals.

_____

- A "5" is where you're paying attention to subconscious MindStories that run you, taking steps everyday to re-write the limiting ones to be more empowering. You're hardly ever reactive and you make more empowering choices each day.
- A "4" is where you're paying attention to subconscious MindStories that run you, and take steps every week to make them more empowering. What used to knock you down for a long time now only affects you for a few minutes.
- A "3" is average. It depends on the circumstances. Some things you can let go of immediately; whereas, other things you just cannot seem to shake off. It's very much hit and miss.
- A "2" is below average. This is where you seem to get easily reactive. You're not making many empowering choices.
- A "1" is where you're constantly at the mercy of external circumstances. You give up very easily, and feel totally stuck.

5. On a scale of 1 to 5, rate your level of ATTENTION and ability to focus on a goal to the exclusion of all opposition _____

- A "5" is where you're at the Super Achiever level and you mostly hear empowering Self Talk. You can focus on your goals to the exclusion of any opposition that comes your way. You seem to effortlessly achieve your biggest goals.
- A "4" is where you're playing at your best about 70% to 80% of the time and can see consistently good results from your efforts. You mostly hear empowering Self Talk inside your head, and quickly turn around limiting Self Talk.
- A "3" is average. You're easily distracted. You seem to find it difficult to stay focused on important tasks. You're just busy being busy. Disempowering Self Talk fills your head about 50% of the time.
- A "2" is where you're just overwhelmed most of the time. You struggle to get anything done on your task list. Disempowering Self Talk fills your head about 75% of the time.
- A "1" is where you seem to be just caught in the victim mindset. You're constantly focusing on what's not happening, on what's not great in your life. Disempowering Self Talk fills your head about 80-100% of the time.

6. On a scale of 1 to 5 how much MOMENTUM do you have in your business and life right now? _____

- A "5" is a world class level. You have so much momentum, you cannot stop your success even if you wanted to.
- A "4" is excellent. You have momentum. Things are moving in the right direction in your life and you're on track with your goals. Occasionally, you feel the wind deflate your sails, but you course correct and keep going.
- A "3" is average level. Your results have plateaued and haven't really changed much over the last six months.

- A "2" is below average. You have very little momentum and often have to start over.
- A "1" is where you have no momentum whatsoever. You feel stuck with no options.

7. On a scale of 1 to 5, how effective are you at putting new HABITS into place and sticking to them? _____

- A "5" is ninja level. The right actions are in place, so much so that you don't even have to think about them. That's the definition of a habit - your actions are on automatic pilot.
- A "4" is where you've put new habits into place although you still need to consciously "will" yourself to keep them up.
- A "3" is average. You've got good habits and bad habits, but the bad habits are sabotaging the good habits.
- A "2" is where you're struggling. Every time you try to put something new in place, it never seems to last and you end up quitting.
- A "1" is where you need A LOT of help. Your reactive patterns and negative programming stop you from even trying.

GRAND TOTAL _____

SCORING

If you scored 29-35: Awesome! You're in a great place and are already achieving much of what you want in life. This book will help you continue to stay on the leading edge.

If you scored 22-28: That is still great because most of the time you're moving towards the life of your dreams and you have generated some seriously good momentum. This book will help you jump up to the next level.

If you scored 15-21: You know what to do some of the time, but you're just not doing what you know. There will be times that you start to see results, but then it will all come crashing down as you sabotage yourself. If you put a lot more focus on the processes and support in this book, you'll find your score going up.

If you scored 8-14: You have a little bit of hope that keeps you from totally giving up; but most days your belief level is low and you take very few risks. Commit to applying yourself fully to the tools and techniques in this book and you'll find things changing for the better soon.

If you scored 0-7: then life is a struggle and you're likely in a dark place. In the hero's journey, they would call this the 'abyss'. The fact is, we've all been there at times, and we're all meant to go through those 'dark nights of the soul'. It's part of the process. Commit to applying yourself fully to the tools and techniques in this book, you'll find this time of darkness will reveal it's gifts -- leading you back home more quickly.

INTERPRETATION

No matter what level you are at, this book can help you break free of any place you're stuck. Congratulations for being honest with yourself. That is always the first step to making things better.

Getting your MINDSTORIES right can help you take action from an inspired, connected place where you can start to see results FAST. You're going to learn how to reprogram yourself, so that nothing stops you from reaching the life you were meant to live. Are you ready for your next level? Great! Turn the page and let's get started!

Section 1

ACCEPTANCE

ACCEPTANCE

ACCEPTANCE is Part 1 of the AVARA Coaching Model. This is where you explore, accept and shift your interpretation of life experiences.

This is a great place to start if you have some form of fear going on or if you're worried, anxious, concerned or nervous. You might hear yourself say something like:

> *I feel like something is blocking me, but I'm not sure what it is.*
> *I'm anxious about an upcoming deadline.*
> *I am concerned about other people's opinions.*
> *I am worrying about money.*

ACCEPTANCE is about:

- accepting where you are right now in terms of negative feelings
- being able to identify the interpretations behind those feelings
- choosing new thoughts that create a more empowering MindStory

Many people don't want to acknowledge or feel their emotions and so they end up suppressing, distracting or projecting them. Then the feelings OWN you, instead of the other way around. For example, body imbalances are often a sign of *suppressing* your feelings (e.g. tension, health issues, moodiness). Addictions are often a sign of *distractimg* yourself from feelings (e.g. food, alcohol, drugs, overworking, etc.) Being reactive and blaming is often a sign of *projecting* your feelings onto outside circumstances or people.

Accepting the things you cannot control in life is the first step in the process of transformation. It also helps you to create the feelings and meanings that will transform the situation. In the empowering MindStory column you'll use the words **"I have chosen to be…"**. This is an instruction set to the subconscious mind to switch. Even though you don't feel those positive emotions yet, you are creating a field into which that's now possible. It also reminds you that you choose all your feelings, all the time, negative or positive. Try the model below on your own issue. When stating negative "meanings" list as many as come to mind, even if they **seem silly, strange or unlikely**. Often the meanings come from a childlike part of yourself. While they may be hard to accept at first, you need to in order to grow.

Step A – Issue: What's a problem in your life? Describe the situation. No editing. We'll refer to this as your Limiting MindStory.

E.g. I'm not getting enough new customers because I don't know where to find them. For example, last month I only got 5 new customers when I really need 25. I just doubt I'll be able to get 25, so I'm settling for what I think I can get. I'm not that excited about the goal, but it's better than nothing, right?

Step B – Facts: Now state what you wrote above as objectively as possible. Separate facts from your interpretation - no adjectives, adverbs, descriptive phrases, feelings or opinions. From an outside perspective what would everyone agree on?

E.g. Last month I got 5 new customers.

Step C – Limiting Story	**Step D – Empowering Story**
Now, you're going to break your MindStory down into its components parts here in the "Limiting Story" section. Then, we'll transform it in the "Empowering Story" section in the right-hand column. Start by going down this left column first, then go on to Step D, in the right-hand column.	Now that you've broken down your MindStory into its components parts, we'll transform it in this "Empowering Story" section. Look at what you wrote in each of the parts in the left column, and create a positive version here.

1) Acceptance: What are the limiting feelings, thoughts and meaning you are giving to the situation? Express it like this *I'm* (negative feeling) *because* (negative thought). *I'm feeling this way because I'm making this situation mean...* (your interpretation).

E.g. **I'm feeling** doubtful about being successful, **because** I'm not getting enough customers to generate a positive cash flow. **I'm making this mean** that I'm not skilled enough, and without a good enough offer to run my own business.

I AM FEELING
_____
_____
_____

BECAUSE
_____
_____
_____

I'M MAKING THIS MEAN (list all, even if they seem unlikely or silly)
_____
_____
_____

1) Acceptance: What are more empowering feelings, thoughts and meanings you could give to the situation? Express it like this *I have chosen to be* (positive feeling) *because* (positive thought). *A better meaning I could give this situation is...*

E.g. **I have chosen to** believe in myself and my abilities **because** I'm willing to learn. **A better meaning is** that I have something of real value that people want. If I can enroll 5, I can enroll 25. If I think bigger, I'll enjoy the journey far more.

I HAVE CHOSEN TO BE
_____
_____
_____

BECAUSE
_____
_____
_____

A BETTER MEANING (that would feel more empowering to you)
_____
_____
_____

2) Vision: What is your possible future A YEAR FROM NOW if you live from this limiting MindStory? Be specific. *E.g. At this rate a year from now, l will have maxed out my credit and will have to go back to a job or end up homeless.*	**2) Vision:** What is your possible future A YEAR FROM NOW if you live from this more empowering MindStory? Be specific. *E.g. l will easily be generating 25 customers or more per month. My revenue will exceed my expenses and I'll be living my vision.*
3) Action: What action or inaction is taking place? *E.g. I'm procrastinating on taking the actions I should be taking.*	**3) Action:** What actions could you take to achieve this empowering VISION? Anything goes. No editing. List at least 7 ideas. Then choose 1 idea and break it down to specific, small, next steps in Step E below. *E.g. I'm going to consistently phone 10 people a day* 1. 2. 3. 4. 5. 6. 7.

4) Reprogram: What is a recent event or experience that triggered this issue? Use present tense as if you were there now. *E.g. I'm about to start phoning potential customers for the day. Very quickly, self-doubt kicks in and I find myself feeling completely hopeless and uninspired about the possibility of even getting 1 new customer, let alone 5 or 25.*	**4) Reprogram:** What is a similar event or experience that might happen in the near future where it's playing out in a more empowering way? Use present tense as if you were there now. *E.g. I'm about to start phoning potential customers for the day. I'm maintaining my vision, feeling confident, certain and inspired about the possibility of getting 25 customers or more. I easily make 10 calls and it's so much fun.*
5) Attention: What are the limiting beliefs here or negative Self Talk? List all, even if they seem mean-spirited, unlikely or silly? *E.g. I just don't know what I'm doing. I don't have what it takes to make this happen. Who would want to buy from me? What's the point of even trying to contact people and interest them in what I have to offer? They're just going to say 'NO' anyway.*	**5) Attention:** What might be your new beliefs or Self Talk from this more empowering MindStory? Start your sentence with this progressive affirmation: "Every day in every way I'm…" *E.g. Every day in every way I'm becoming better and better at connecting with people in a way that makes them excited to become my customer.*

Step E - Specific Next Actions: Pick one idea from your empowering ACTION section above. What are 1 to 3 specific, small, next steps to get that started? Give each a date, delegate where possible. By breaking down big goals into small steps, it makes them feel easier to accomplish.

#	Action	Who	When
Eg	*Follow up with 10 people who expressed interest in my product in the last 3 months*	Me	Tuesday
1.			
2.			
3.			

CHAPTER 1

You Are What You Feel

*What lies behind us and what lies before us are tiny
matters compared to what lies within us.*
– Ralph Waldo Emerson

DAVE'S STORY

Remember in the introduction when I was driving like a maniac, and I was late for work? I came to a roundabout and hit the brakes to slow down, but the car did not slow down because the brakes failed. I was speeding towards one of Dublin's busiest roundabouts with cars coming into it from all directions! My life suddenly flashed before my eyes. (Yes, that does happen). The decisions I'd made, the roles I chose to play, the stories I'd chosen to live by. It wasn't pretty. I was convinced this was the end. In that split second, I decided to let go and hand myself over to the divine. What else could I do? And then, something extraordinary happened. A miracle of sorts. I experienced a moment of extreme clarity and expanded awareness. Somehow, I felt completely safe and looked after. I felt supported, as if the Universe had my back.

Inexplicably, all the cars entering the roundabout managed to avoid colliding with me. Something came in and created a space around me and protected me. I know it sounds other worldly, but that's the only way I can describe it. I miraculously made it through the roundabout unscathed and pulled over into the hard shoulder about a quarter of a mile ahead. I was breathing heavily and my heart was pounding. I started crying with relief. It was truly a wake-up call from the Universe. Life was giving me a second chance. I vowed, there and then, to set a new course for my future.

What happened next was amazing…I'll tell you later.

EVERYTHING YOU DO IN YOUR LIFE IS BECAUSE YOU WANT TO FEEL A CERTAIN WAY

Successful people understand that when they set big exciting goals, it's because they want to feel a certain way. Think about it. Why do we ultimately want to be successful or achieve our greatest vision? Often, it's not so much the result, but it's how the result makes us feel.

And the problem is that nobody teaches us this. They don't pull us aside and say, "Okay, here is the deal. Everything you want in your life is because of how you want to feel." Think about it. If one of your goals is financial freedom, why do you want to achieve this? It's because it will make you feel like a success. You'll feel secure. You'll feel happy or fulfilled or peaceful or free. Perhaps you'll feel proud or significant or grateful. Maybe all of these. It's the feelings that you think you will have in achieving the result or the feelings you think you will avoid in not getting it.

In addition, every positive and negative feeling is a direct result of our thoughts. It's impossible to feel unhappy without first having unhappy thoughts. It's impossible to feel lonely without having lonely thoughts.

Each thought you have, your consciousness turns into a sensory experience. It's easy to forget that you choose to think those thoughts. Often the thoughts are happening below our conscious awareness. Many of your thoughts may not be serving you. Most people think that it's the external circumstances of their lives that create how they feel, but really, it's their thinking that's determining whether they feel positive or negative, happy or unhappy, a success or a failure.

For example, Anne promotes her first seminar. She books a big room hoping for 100 people to attend. Only 15 people show up. Most of them are friends and family. The fact of this situation is that she had expectations that were not met. At that point, she has a choice about how to interpret those facts. One possible interpretation is, "I'm a failure," "People don't like me," "I'm just not cut out for this." She's takes the low road. As a result, she feels embarrassed, humiliated, disappointed, frustrated, angry, hurt and dejected. She ruminates on this situation and on past failures night and day for weeks. This leads to inaction. She decides to never put on a seminar again. Her business grinds to a halt.

Here's an alternative scenario she could have played out. Anne promotes her first seminar. She books a big room hoping for 100 people to attend. Only 15 people show up. Most of them are friends and family. She takes the high road, by making a different choice about how to interpret those facts, by telling herself, "I'm ok, regardless of attendance," "There are people who do like me," "I'm absolutely meant to do this," "Next time I could learn how to market the event in better ways." As a result, she feels at peace, curious, inspired and confident to try again. She focuses on reaching out to the people who did attend, and on how to do it better next time. This leads to good action. She decides to try again. Her business keeps going. Eventually, she gets better and fills up her seminars with 100 people and more.

From the outside, her response in the first scenario seems silly and neurotic. That said, even people who have done years of coaching, personal growth, self-esteem building and success seminars can still fall into that trap. Why is it so hard for most people to take the high road?

WE CAN BECOME ADDICTED TO NEGATIVE EMOTIONS

According to Neuroscience the brain doesn't care if you take the high road or the low road. What DOES it care about? Efficiency. Whatever you focus on grows. Whatever you feed the brain, it wants to become good at that. It will seek proficiency. Therefore, if you choose the low road, you repeatedly reinforce the neural circuitry of that thought and get stuck within the experience of that past emotion, like a record caught in a groove. Not only that, but you can become addicted to the chemicals that negative emotions release into the body. It's like getting addicted to drugs.

For example, you may know people who seem to continually create drama in their life. They actually seem to like the negative emotions. It's true. They do. In fact, trying to change your emotional pattern from negative to positive is like going through drug withdrawal. That's why so many people find it difficult to change. We become a slave to the process because it's all happening on automatic pilot.

Therefore, if your emotions are caused by your thoughts, and everything you do in your life is in order to feel better, wouldn't it be important to have more control over your thoughts and feelings? It absolutely would.

One of the most common questions you could ask yourself every day is, "How can I generate more positive emotions NOW that I would feel if I actually achieved my dream?"

This seems counterintuitive to many people, but that's how high achievers manifest their goals. They actually practice feeling the emotions they would feel if they achieved their goal. For example, while Anne was marketing her seminar, she could have imagined how she would feel if 100 people attended. She could imagine seeing the room with every seat taken, engaged people listening, all the logistics going smoothly, and her seminar making a big difference for everyone.

Therefore, it makes her feel happy, grateful, good about herself, and confident. It's those feelings that reinforce new neural circuitry and a different chemical reaction in her body. She then gets addicted to feeling happy, grateful, good about herself, and confident. Therefore, she naturally chooses thoughts and takes actions that help her to feel more of that. Then her capacity, ingenuity, persistence and personal power all rise. It's a domino effect in either direction. Strange but true.

If you can get yourself into those positive emotions more frequently, then you can get those results more often. Does that make sense?

START THINKING AND FEELING PURPOSEFULLY

The way to unravel bad habits of mind is to start thinking and interpreting by choice. It's a new way of being for many people, and so it will feel uncomfortable at first. It's like going to the gym and trying to lift a weight when your muscles are weak. But, if you persist, you eventually become stronger and the rewards are phenomenal.

If you understand that thinking is a choice rather than something outside of your control, then it helps you to dismiss negative thoughts that pass through your mind. You can imagine hitting the "delete" key, and seeing them erased. Thoughts are things. Even though we can't see them, they have a definite electrical and magnetic charge. Therefore, you can grow them or delete them. All great inventions, art, buildings – started with a thought. They are the building blocks of life. Use them wisely. They don't own you. You own them.

They create your reality. If a thought enters your mind that creates a reality you don't want, you have full permission to deny it entry. If you receive a spam email about a product that you don't want, why would you open the email and read the whole thing? That's what people often do with negative thoughts. They think their thoughts represent reality, when in actuality they are just a possibility that you can choose to focus on or not.

There's a massive difference in believing that your thoughts are real or that your thoughts are just thoughts. We think about something, and we feel the effects of our thoughts.

It's the same with your feelings. Negative feelings are no more a representation of reality than positive feelings. They are both just possibilities. They are like colors on your artist's palette. You can paint your life with dull grey and medium black, or with vibrant green and lively turquoise. In short, it is your thoughts and not your circumstances that determine how you feel.

Remember this the next time you feel bad. Trace it back to the thought that's running in the background. Then, it's easy to make the switch and that's exactly what high achievers do.

As such, they tend to view setbacks and failure as mere feedback. They simply reframe the experience and lock straight onto their goals again. They stay in the feel-good zone for longer periods of time.

WHAT WE CAN AND CANNOT CONTROL

There are many things in the world that we have no control over. We cannot control other people, our past or things that have happened to us; but we do have control over how we think about those things and how we interpret what they mean.

I believe that everything happens for a reason…sometimes we can't see it right away. Sometimes life gets a little more difficult than we want it to. But ultimately, we have this great blessing to have control over our destiny by choosing how we're going respond to things.

Think about how you've been feeling the last few months or years. Were you generally happy, peaceful, fulfilled, or were you mostly unhappy, stressed and unfulfilled? We all go up and down, but was there a dominant pattern? The reality is you were choosing to feel this way. It's important to realize that it's always a choice. Alternatively, were you blaming the economy, the government, other people or external circumstances for your negative feelings? Your responses, your actions or non-actions have shaped your life today and where you have ended up.

Nobody can bring you peace but yourself.
— *Ralph Waldo Emerson*

That's why here at MindStory Academy we spend a lot of time training our students to progressively take greater control of their thoughts, so they can generate more of the feelings that will support the actions they want to take and bring about the results they ultimately want to achieve.

OBSERVING YOUR THOUGHTS

Please note that this doesn't mean that you will never have negative thoughts again. It's about the ability to observe your thoughts and the feelings they create. Then, you get to decide how you're going to respond to them. That takes some practice, especially if you've spent a few decades not observing and not exercising choice. But, the good news is that anyone can rebuild this essential life skill.

It usually starts with accepting the negative feelings and allowing them space in your body-mind consciousness. It's usually only then that you can trace back the feelings to thoughts, usually looping in your subconscious mind. At that point, you can decide, "Is this something I want to continue to think, or not?" If not, then you can refocus on what you DO want to think and feel.

Conversely, when you either resist and suppress the negative feelings or go into a reactive state, then you can become locked in, building a chemical addiction to that negative state. That's why many of us deep down feel anxious, unworthy, agitated or frustrated a lot of the time. Even though you may not like those states of mind, there's a subconscious chemical addiction going on. They are deeper reactive patterns. By not facing the feelings, you can never get to the unconscious thoughts that drive them.

Once we become consciously aware, it becomes much easier to transform the thought and therefore the feeling so you can respond with a better choice. When you do this inner work, you begin to release negative emotions that have been trapped in your unconscious going back years. If you are willing to feel any negative emotion, you're not going to be so freaked out by the negative thoughts when they appear in your mind. You can look at them from a neutral place, learn from them, and let them go.

SO YOU THINK YOU'RE A POSITIVE PERSON?

The problem is that most people don't like to identify themselves as a person who thinks negative thoughts, or who has negative feelings. At the conscious level, they may in fact think they are "positive thinkers", non-reactive and calm. They're convinced they don't suppress anything, but the symptoms are there, such as stress-related health issues like restless sleep, poor digestion, or low immunity.

In addition, when not facing that aspect of themselves they'll distract themselves with overeating, alcohol, recreational drugs, pharmaceutical drugs, shopping, caffeine, entertainment, gambling, overworking, etc. In fact, they'll try anything to get a dopamine rush in high hopes of drowning out the negativity. But if the root cause of the negativity has not been addressed, it all comes rushing back soon after and often gets worse, as the cycle repeats itself. In other words, trying to get rid of the negativity with avoidance actually helps grow it.

A good way to know if this is happening to you is to pay attention to how you're feeling. Let yourself feel those feelings in your body – the agitation, anxiety, frustration, sadness, hurt, disappointment. Then see if you can trace it back to looping thoughts about yourself that are running in the background. For example, many people, even highly successful people, discover that when they really pay attention, they are noticing thoughts such as:

> *I'm not good enough*
> *I'm never going to amount to anything*
> *I'm a failure*
> *I'm an imposter*
> *I don't know what I'm doing*
> *Other people are better than me*
> *People don't like me or care about me*

If you discover any of those thoughts, greet them with compassion and curiosity. Don't try to fight them or do a counter argument just yet with that judgmental side of you, as that will only grow them. Treat them like you would a crying toddler who's seeking attention. Be compassionate with yourself without buying into the drama. Often those looping thoughts are not the real you; they are programs you picked up years ago. You can learn how to delete them.

FEELING NEGATIVE EMOTIONS

There are instances in your life when you're going to want to choose to feel a negative emotion. That's part of the human experience. For example, if you feel sad about losing a pet, you need to feel that. If you feel upset about someone speaking to you in a disrespectful way, or if you feel angry about environmental pollution— sometimes, those are the ways you want to feel. They are natural and a healthy expression of being human.

The problem comes when you get stuck there. We have a large patio outside our office on the penthouse floor, where birds come to find food in the little garden there. Often two birds will go for the same piece of food at the same time, like a crow and a seagull. One gets the food, and the other squawks and flaps its wings in frustration. Then it seems to go back to a state of serenity and keeps on hunting for food. That, I believe, is the more natural way we are meant to feel and express emotions. Feel them, and release them. Instead, many people partially feel them, suppress them, get reactive, then judge their reaction. An inner war happens where the emotion never really gets a chance to be felt and released. For big issues, maybe it needs to be felt and released a few times, but eventually it will pass.

When you only partially experience negative emotions like fear and anger, you actually stay stuck there for long periods of time. I'm sure you know people who seem to be almost always stuck under a cloud of anger, anxiety, sadness or fear. They need to do an emotional cleanse and start the process of experiencing the full range of emotions that life has to offer. Once you can cultivate that habit, you tend to feel more of the heartfelt positive emotions because this is your true nature. Emotions such as gratitude, joy, excitement, enthusiasm, fascination, awe, inspiration, wonder, trust, appreciation, kindness, passion, and empowerment. These are the types of emotions that let you truly create a life you love.

THE SECRET TO MANIFESTING YOUR GOALS

The paradox of living is to be happy with yourself in the present moment while also maintaining a dream of your ideal future. This is the ultimate secret for manifestation. We are often programed to get frustrated when our dreams haven't manifested. We wish things were different and get frustrated when we haven't yet accomplished an important goal. The problem is that an attitude of frustration can actually prevent the goal from manifesting.

For example, when I was first starting my business, I tried all kinds of things to create income, and very little of it worked. My debt was growing. I felt frustrated and unhappy and longed for the day when I would have a successful business so that I would feel secure inside and happy. The problem was that my frustration and unhappiness were blocking the success of my business. I needed to feel secure and happy first and THEN things started to take off.

When you feel present, inspired and whole that you no longer care whether your goal will happen, you become detached from the outcome and that's when amazing things materialize before your eyes. We've seen this time and time again with our clients from around the world who take control of their thoughts and feelings.

You feel so complete that you no longer feel a lack of something, and you no longer try to do it all by yourself. You let go, and to your amazement, something greater responds and you laugh at the simplicity of the process.

HOW TO DEAL WITH NEGATIVE PEOPLE

A question we are frequently asked is: "How do I deal with negative people?" I've heard this more times than I can count. "Every time I'm around this person they pull me into their negativity." Often, they even blame the negative people around them as the reason why they're not succeeding.

If you have experienced this, then stop to consider this for a minute. What most people don't realize is that when we blame someone for our circumstances today, we give away our power to that person. As a result, we give away our power and ability to change. What you are actually saying here is that somebody else is responsible for the way you feel about anything.

Therefore, the ultimate question you need to ask is: "Am I in control here or am I allowing other people or external circumstances to control me?

Consider how you want to show up in the relationship – business or personal. You need to start taking control of your thoughts. If a person or circumstance triggers a negative reaction in you, then chances are it's just activating something already inside you. Conversely, have you ever heard someone complain about another person you know, and yet that person doesn't bother you at all? It's the old saying: *We don't see the world as it is; we see the world as we are.*

TAKING BACK YOUR POWER

Let's take the metaphor of planting a garden. Consciously choosing the emotional state you want is like planting flowers in your garden, and then ensuring they get water, fertilizer and sunshine. It also means clearing away the weeds. Many people allow weeds [negative emotions and thoughts] to overrun the garden of their mind.

This work is about becoming aware of what you're thinking, and it's about understanding your habitual thought patterns. When you can start

recognizing, "I react this way because of what I'm thinking and feeling, NOT because of what the person is doing," that can change everything for the better. That awareness, in and of itself, is a huge turning point in taking back control over your thoughts.

That said, this is only the first step. Once you become aware of your thinking and feeling patterns and how you're reacting to them, the next step becomes catching yourself BEFORE you react.

When you recognize that something is just a thought that produces a feeling, and not something you have to react to, that's when you can start changing disempowering behavioral patterns.

The next step is to start deciding that you want to think purposefully. Ask yourself: *What are the emotional states that I am going to bring to a challenging situation in my life?*

For example, if lack of cash flow and too much debt is an issue, it's easy to spend your creative energy in worry. What if you brought compassion, enthusiasm and curiosity to the situation? That seems counterintuitive. Yet, those feelings would actually create the space into which you can far more easily solve the situation, rather than through worry. Then you create the thoughts that would help you feel those feelings such as, "It's ok that I've made financial mistakes. That's the way I learn. I'm eager to learn how to better handle cash flow situations. I'm curious to find a solution that will work. It's an interesting challenge."

IN CONCLUSION

In conclusion, when things do not go as planned, successful people focus on the thoughts and emotions that support the direction they're going in. They reconnect to their goals, take on board the feedback, process the lessons, make the necessary changes and set off again.

You can do the same, and we've broken it down in a way that makes it easy to do. The variable that will determine your success at doing this is simply your ability to manage your state of mind by taking control of your thoughts and feelings.

We can't control other people; nor can we control our past because it's already done. We can't control external circumstances happening out there in the world. But, what we can control are our thoughts, our emotions, our actions and ultimately our results. All of those things are within our control; and when you really get that, your entire life changes.

HOMEPLAY

1) Choose 3 positive emotions that you want to feel more of during your day. Then, choose a really exciting goal that you think about every day. Look at the goal every day and tell yourself, "That's what I want you primarily to focus on. And these are the 3 emotions I want to generate."

These are the feelings I want to generate more of today:

a) _____

b) _____

c) _____

Our imagination can be used for either anxiety or creativity. We're either worrying about something that creates anxiety for ourselves, or we're creating something.

If you direct your mind in a way that's thinking about creation, that's thinking about a goal or a future you want to have, you're using your imagination and your mind is working for you instead of against you.

2) Ask yourself better questions. "How can I feel amazing today? How can I help more people today? How can I add more value in the world today? What can I think today that will create the 3 positive emotions I want to feel more of?" When you ask your mind these types of questions, it can't

help but find a positive empowering answer. And it causes your brain to focus on what's great about where you are or where you're going.

Most people ask themselves the wrong questions such as, "Why am I so tired? Why am I so stupid? Why am I such a loser?" If you ask yourself those questions, you will generate the negative thoughts and feelings that disempower you and move you further away from your goals.

Questions like, "What do I have to be thankful for? What level of focus am I at right now? How can I create more magic moments today?" Those are questions that will upgrade your mindset, increase your confidence and move you closer to your dream.

3) Relax, close your eyes and think of a time in your past when you felt super confident. Concentrate on a specific event, fully return to that time now and step into your body. Remember what you saw at the time; immerse yourself into the positive memory. What did you hear? What did you say to yourself during the experience? Relive the amazing feeling of confidence you had at that time.

Turn the memory up a notch, make it brighter, bigger, bolder, really feel those positive, confident emotions in your body and in your mind. Make the sounds louder and clearer and the colors richer and more vivid. You want to relive this event with as much detail and positive emotional intensity as possible.

As you think these good thoughts and feel these good feelings, squeeze the thumb and middle finger of either hand together.

Still holding your thumb and finger together, think about a situation in your future in which you want to feel confident and unstoppable.

Imagine things going perfectly, going exactly the way you want them to go. See what you see, hear the sounds and add in the feelings, feeling how great it is to achieve the result you desire. Do this for 15-20 seconds, then let go of your thumb and middle finger.

Practice this every day and soon just squeezing your thumb and middle finger together will trigger positive feelings of confidence, certainty and conviction. Your mind is very sensitive and will photograph these states. You will believe more and more in your vision; and each time you go through this process your ability to perform in the real world will increase.

This is how you influence and start taking control of your emotional states. You no longer have to be a victim of circumstance, at the mercy of other people's actions, or held back by your past experiences.

CHAPTER 2

How to End Self-Sabotage

Most people lead lives of quiet desperation. They hide an unconscious despair
under the typical amusements of the day. This despair is born of giving
up too soon. Most people go to the grave with their song still in them.
– Henry David Thoreau

CARLA'S STORY

In the first year of starting my business, I needed some help in my office. I contacted a Job Club that helped people acquire job skills. Through them, I arranged for a practicum student for three months, full-time. My job was to give this person marketable job skills in exchange for free help.

Helen arrived for her first day of work late, wearing an oversized sweatshirt with a big 'happy face' on it, baby stains down the front, hair askew, and smelling of talcum powder. She told me she was a single parent of three and was only 21 years old. She had been a runaway and a drop out at thirteen, soon after which she became pregnant. All she knew was how to take care of babies.

She knew nothing about computers or office work, so each day took a lot of explaining. Her second day there she permanently deleted an important document I'd been working on, by mistake. The next day she spilled coffee all over the computer keyboard, which fried it completely. Each time she made a mistake she looked ready to cry. Clearly, she was sabotaging herself. I didn't have the heart to reprimand her. On the fourth day, I saw her ready to cry again because she had somehow broken the three-hole punch.

I decided to try something with her that I'd been using with my clients. I said, "Let's try this thing – just for fun. We each get this notepad called the 'Way to Go' pad. If I catch you doing something right, I'll make a note of appreciation about it. You do the same for me."

She rolled her eyes and replied, "Good luck finding something for me."

The next day I was waiting for her to arrive, so we could start this project. When she showed up 45 minutes late, I wrote a note – *You showed up!* She laughed. Later that day, I wrote her another note for organizing my shelf of supplies neatly. These notes seemed to help her calm down. Eventually, she built up some basic skills.

I was giving her the most positive feedback about her people skills, so I let her take messages for me. One day when I was out, she took a call from a prospective client. They hit it off right away, talking about how to soothe teething problems with kids.

She built such great rapport with this woman, that by the time I got back, Helen had booked a speaking engagement for me. I was amazed and so was she. I put her straight onto client relations. After 3 months, she had to leave and she moved on to her next assignment. I gave her a glowing reference letter, and a big hug.

Five years later, I was walking in downtown Vancouver and a woman walked by wearing an haute couture grey suit with crimson piping, hair pulled up in a French knot, carrying a leather briefcase and talking on her cell phone. It was Helen.

Apparently, she had worked her way up in a public relations firm and was now able to support her family and get off welfare. As we chatted, she told me that she still carried around the 'Way to Go' notes I gave her years back. She actually pulled them all out of her briefcase. The light blue notes were crumpled up and covered in coffee stains. She said they were also tinged with tear stains. On bad days, she would read these notes, especially this one...*You showed up!* It was the first time she'd been in an environment where positive reinforcement was the norm. The notes helped her keep going and break through the self-sabotage. She went on to use them with her kids and they loved them. She also used them with her colleagues at her PR firm.

I was amazed at how an activity that took me a few minutes a day had such a big ripple effect, not only on one person's life but also on so many others.

HOW CHANGING YOUR SELF-TALK CHANGES YOUR LIFE

I hear this over and over again from my clients. "Carla, I know what to do to grow my business. I'm just not doing what I know." Every time I ask one of my clients to fill out a questionnaire to find out what's holding them back, a lack of consistent action is always right up there at the top.

Why don't we take the actions that we know we need to take to become successful?

It's so frustrating, isn't it? So, why don't we take the actions that we know we need to take to become successful?

What's stopping you?

Is there some self-sabotage going on?

Self-sabotage is defined as creating unnecessary problems for yourself, interfering with your own progress and your own goals.

It's very common for people who are growing a business, or building their career to feel like it's impossible to achieve their goals. They feel like giving up.

They want to quit.

They believe that they're not good enough, not worthy enough.

Ironically, this is often the beginning of their transformation.

Why? Because the sky is always darkest before the dawn. Usually, just before a breakthrough, every possible obstacle inside and out seems to come at you.

The trickiest obstacle at that point in the game is the self-sabotage that's hidden and happening below the threshold of your own conscious awareness.

Self-sabotage is those looping thoughts designed to damage your belief in yourself, increasing your self-doubt and knocking your confidence in hopes it will cause you to give up.

WHAT DOES SELF-SABOTAGE FEEL LIKE?

It can look like inner conflict, tiredness, stress and worry. It's like you're an imposter or a fraud…like you're unworthy of success. If you could watch yourself on video, you might see it. It can affect your tone of voice, your posture and facial expressions – dulling everything down. Some people are in a state of self-sabotage most of the time so they don't know that this is NOT a natural state. What's natural is to feel inner harmony, in the creative flow and worthy of success. For many people, these are just fleeting feelings right after an accomplishment, and then they go right back to a feeling of pressure, inner conflict, agitation and anxiety. Yet, those good feelings are actually your birthright. That's how you felt as a child before you were programmed to doubt your worth. The trick is to recapture that naturally ability and live from that place most of the time.

As we said in the last chapter, self-sabotage is a negative program that isn't the real you. It's akin to a bad virus you inadvertently download onto your *bio-computer*. As you try to launch programs in your bio-computer, the virus corrupts your progress. The problem is that people think the virus is a reflection of who they really are. That's a falsehood. It's a program that many people in society seem to have picked up, from every walk of life. It gets downloaded in subtle and not-so-subtle ways from parents, teachers, advertisements, entertainment, and more. Its purpose is to keep you small and only performing at a small percentage of your capacity. This program aggressively works to kill your hopes, dreams and fondest desires.

My question for you is this: If self-sabotage is not messing around, why on earth should you?

The good news is that you can deconstruct and delete it, like you would delete malware from your laptop. As soon as you know it's there, you can remove it and finally free up your capacity. It may require removing it several times, in several ways, especially if the program has been able to propagate for several decades so far. But, the sooner you begin, the better.

Self-sabotage is a negative subconscious program that isn't the real you.

Be willing to face it head on and see it for what it is. In part, this means being AS committed to achieving your goals and dreams as self-sabotage is to ruining your life.

DECONSTRUCTING SELF-SABOTAGE

Self-sabotage is as dumb as it is powerful. Even though it resides below the threshold of our conscious awareness, when you track it back to its lair and begin to consciously understand it better, you can begin to dissolve it. It leaves clues and has a working game plan that can be broken down and overcome. There are four self-defeating elements of self-sabotage. Most people have some form of these characteristics. The extent to which they result in self-sabotage and interfere with our abilities is only a matter of degree.

1. The Self-Doubt Trigger

Think about a time you considered working on a new goal, the kind of goal that got you excited but that would take you outside your comfort zone. For example, Bill had been a speaker and workshop leader for years. He wanted to put all his material online and create a membership program. That way, he wouldn't have to travel so much. He could work from anywhere. People all over the world, even in remote places, could access his material for a fraction of the price. As soon as he got the idea, the "Self-Doubt Trigger" activated.

> *I don't have what it takes.*
> *It's going to be too much work.*
> *What if people don't like it?*
> *What if I fail?*

This is an aspect of the self-sabotage program that is a kind of booby trap every time you try to break free. It automatically gets triggered. If it has ever happened to you, welcome to the human story. The problem is that people think it's their voice, or a voice of wisdom warning them, trying to help them. The truth is it's just a bad virus you need to remove.

With Bill, I could see what was going on and could point it out to him. Once he saw it, he had the power to break free. You can develop a kind of 'neutral witness' within you that doesn't get caught up in the drama, that doesn't buy into the voice. It just quietly watches the game being played, and then decides not to play. It's the part of you that can reinvest your creative life force energy on the thoughts that make you feel good and on the direction you want to go. Think of it like playing a video game. To win the game, your job is to turn self-doubt into self-belief. In the HOMEPLAY section, you'll see more tools on how to do this.

2. The Unwillingness Trigger

Another booby trap within self-sabotage is the feeling of being unwilling to face struggles, challenges or discomfort. When you raise the bar and want to achieve a larger goal, you will inevitably face struggle, challenges and discomfort. The trick is to catch the 'unwillingness trigger' and redirect your attention.

Here are telltale signs that the 'Unwillingness Trigger' is in effect:

- when you start to procrastinate
- when things don't seem good enough or perfect enough to continue
- when you get distracted by unimportant tasks instead of what's most important
- when you hear yourself complaining about the difficulties of the journey

Overcoming the magnetic pull of this avoidance behavior is not easy…but it can be done and it needs be done if you have any intention of achieving your important goals. You have a choice about this. Every choice you make either builds the power and strength of the self-sabotage program or it builds your natural, true, sovereign self. Again, think of it like a game.

For example, with Bill, he started to recognize the 'Unwillingness Trigger'. Since he liked to go to the gym, I used the metaphor of lifting weights. If you want to build stronger muscles, you need to lift heavier weights. Sometimes life brings larger challenges to overcome because you need more inner strength. By facing the challenge head on instead of avoiding it, you get to build the muscle, which you will need in order to go on your journey. Every time obstacles appeared on his path, he committed to seeing them as opportunities for character development and strength building, instead of a sign he should quit.

Make that commitment to yourself. Practice choosing to transform the 'Unwillingess Trigger' when obstacles or challenges come your way, and instead focus on the rewards that are waiting on the other side. Eventually you'll override it and the neural pathway of "Unwillingness" will fade away from lack of use.

3. The Distraction Trigger

Self-sabotage loves to steal your focus by distracting you with unnecessary and irrelevant activity. It will try to convince you that you are obligated to put your focus there instead of on your important goal. It will give you logical arguments for this that make perfect sense, too.

Here are telltale signs that that 'Distraction Trigger' is in effect. You decide to focus on your important goal and then:

- you say yes to volunteer jobs you don't want to do
- you say yes to social events that you don't want to go to
- you focus on low priority activities like reorganizing your paper-clip drawer
- you get drawn to addictive behavior like binge watching Netflix, going down the social media rabbit hole, overeating, smoking, overdrinking, porn, gambling or shopping
- someone in your life seems to need all your attention all of a sudden

That's when it helps to develop a long 'NO' list and just have a short 'YES' list. Saying NO to any activities that take you away from your goals is the ultimate power move...for it allows you to take ownership of your day, to focus on your highly leveraged actions and to fast-track your goals.

4. The Demotivation Trigger

The 'Demotivation Trigger' shows up as a sudden disinterest in your goals, or a lack of energy. It often shows up greatest at the beginning, when you first set your goal, and right near the finish line. In the beginning, the tactics of self-sabotage are little more than the whispering of a few words of self-doubt. That's all it takes to get most people to give up on their goals, throw in the towel and surrender. It's sad but true as to how little trust people have in themselves and their capacity to figure things out. Then, when the finish line is near, when the last 10% is in sight, that's when the 'Demotivation Trigger' goes into full destructive mode because it knows you're close to completion.

Here are telltale signs that that 'Demotivation Trigger' is in effect. You decide to focus on your important goal and then:

- you suddenly get really tired and have to rest
- your goal now seems unimportant
- you get sick
- an accident or mishap derails your progress

For example, after a year of working on her book, Janice was ready to send everything to the book designer. All of sudden, she got sick, her basement flooded, and her son showed up, out of the blue, asking her to watch his kids for two weeks. These all seem like legitimate distractions, right? She didn't cause them. The interesting thing was, though, that when she decided to keep moving the book forward despite everything, the distractions faded away. She got better quickly, her husband took over dealing with the flood, and her daughter offered to take care of her nieces. If you keep going in whatever way you can, the 'Demotivation Trigger' often de-activates.

That said, be on the alert for another tactic.

Expect self-sabotage right up until completion of your goal, and deal with each one from the place of the neutral witness.

All you need to do is strengthen your resolve. Remember, it's a game, and the ultimate goal is to help you grow.

MAKE A DECISION

We're all playing a high stakes game of life, and if you're ever going to find your greatness, if you're ever going to make your mark on the world… **decide that what you want is more important** than the self-sabotage triggers. Decide that you are 1000x more powerful than the self-sabotage triggers. Once you stand up to it, like standing up to a bully at school, it backs down and goes looking for someone else more fearful to pick on.

You are not the only one struggling with self-sabotage triggers. Most people deal with these triggers…but the high achievers find ways to transform it all and make big things happen.

It's time for you to unleash your greatness and win the game of life.

HOMEPLAY

Try the exercises below and see what you might add to your daily mindset workout.

WAY TO GO NOTES

Keep a small pad of paper next to your bedside or working area. Each time you catch yourself doing something right, something that moves you towards your big goal, make a note of it. You can write anything, big or small. *I worked on my proposal today, I asked my coach for advice, and I made that important call.* Gather the notes in an envelope and reread them whenever you feel lost in a self-sabotage trigger. You can also do this with someone you live or work with, and write out notes for each other. Make a goal of writing at least one note a day for yourself and one for someone else.

POLARITY TO UNITY PROCESS

This is a process adapted from the book, *The Marriage of Spirit*, by Leslie Temple-Thurston. The ego lives in a world of duality: right versus wrong, good versus bad, pleasure versus pain, lack versus abundance, self-sabotage versus self-support.

We tend to go back and forth from one to the other unconsciously, often desiring one and fearing the other. That, of course, keeps us locked in the duality, unable to break free. Without doing a process like this it can take years to transcend the polarities. Here, we'll focus on transcending the duality of self-sabotage versus self-support, which creates an integration of both leading to freedom and growth.

Take a piece of paper and write out your fears and desires for both self-sabotage and self-support when it comes to realizing a specific goal, like growing your business. See the example below. Then try it yourself. You can use the same answers, or come up with your own.

Desire for Self-Support - I am more likely to succeed, I will feel happier, it seems healthier, I move towards my goals more quickly.

Fear of Self-Sabotage - I will get stuck trying to move towards my goals, I am less likely to succeed, I will be more stressed, it seems unhealthy.

Desire for Self-Sabotage - I won't have to deal with the discomfort of growing and realizing my goals, things will stay more familiar, I will not be a target for rejection and failure, I'll stay safer.

Fear of Self-Support - Growing can be uncomfortable, fear of the unfamiliar, more likely to be a target for rejection and failure, it's less safe.

At the end, clasp your hands together to symbolize the unification of the opposites. Think of a transcendant word that you are attracted to such as:

Acceptance

Balance

Clarity

Compassion

Detachment

Equanimity

Flow

Forgiveness

Generosity

Gratitude

Harmony

Humility

Joy

Loyalty

Neutrality

Patience

Selflessness

Surrender

Tolerance

Trust

Truth

Unconditional love

Unity

Wisdom

Then, allow your unconscious to go to work on the integration.

## CHAPTER 3

Believing Without Self-Doubt

'What we are today comes from our thoughts of yesterday, and our present thoughts build our life of tomorrow: our life is the creation of minds.'
– Buddha

DAVE'S STORY

I come from very humble beginnings, no privileged background, no special circumstances. I have experienced great successes in my life. Like many people, I have also walked through the valley of the darkness of disappointment, despair and defeat. I think life lacks adventure and depth without a taste for both.

Growing up, my mother was like an angel in my life, who was always encouraging me to learn new things. She took me to a Transcendental Meditation class when I was 12. I loved it so much that, throughout my teens, when the family was watching TV at night, I'd be in my room meditating.

Fast forward to my university years and I decided to do business studies - not because it spoke to my heart, but because of the advice of others. They suggested that doing this was the fast track to success and fitting in. I never really fit in to begin with, so I quit and started doing Yoga, Personal Development, Tai Chi and Martial Arts.

A lot of people told me that I wouldn't amount to very much, that I didn't have what it takes to be a success and that I would never make the cut.

My big dream was to become world class at speaking, selling and coaching in the area of personal development and wellness. Self-development had made a huge difference to me, and I wanted others to have that, too. A lot of people don't like selling, but I learned to love it because it was about connecting with people in an authentic way, and exploring if what you offered was a good fit for what they needed. It required me to transcend the usual limitations and access a higher state of mind – where literally anything was possible. It also set me on a path of writing my own ticket in life, and creating the life I truly wanted. It forced me to grow in ways I never anticipated.

For example, as I mentioned earlier at 25, I was a struggling salesman. I was very enthusiastic and wanted to succeed in every cell of my body. I worked hard. Often the self-sabotage triggers kicked in. They were like these gremlins on my shoulder always talking me out of my greatness. Unfortunately, after 2 years, I held the record for losing the most amount of money in the company. They called me the worst salesman they had ever seen, which was not exactly a good sign for someone who dreamed of becoming a legendary salesman.

After I survived my brakes failing at the roundabout, I was at a crossroads in my life. I was so frustrated and angry at where I was in my life. Something had to change.

We've all heard the saying, "When the student is ready, the teacher appears." Well, it was my time. Life sent me a great mentor when I needed it most.

Have you ever had someone believe in you more than you believed in yourself? Sometimes that's all it takes, right? My mentor, Tony, shined a light on my true potential. He helped me see that I could achieve the impossible. He taught me to how to use more of my mind - in particular how to reprogram my unconscious mind for success.

I learned how to take charge of my thoughts and emotions. As a result, my life did a complete 180. I went from being the worst salesman in my company to being the best. I developed leadership and influence skills. I overcame my fear of public speaking. Working with Tony was a very magical time in my life. It made the vital difference and gave me the foundation to build the wonderful life I lead today.

HOW TO BELIEVE WITHOUT DOUBT

No truer words have ever been spoken than Henry Ford's: "Whether you believe you can do a thing or not, you are right." You can take all the action in the world, but if you don't believe in yourself and in your ability to succeed, you will struggle to make it happen. Most people think that they believe in themselves because of external events, like winning an award, or making a lot of money. If so, then why are there wealthy people whose walls are lined with awards who still don't believe in themselves? Why are there people with no awards, who do believe in themselves? It's what you decide inside.

The good news is that you can *create* belief in yourself and your offerings to the world. You can literally create belief from nothing. You've already done it many times in life. It's where you suspended disbelief long enough to try something new in life, like asking someone on a date, or applying for a job, or posting your first video online. Become aware of how you did that and duplicate the process. That's what this book is about at its core. We've studied how to practice believing without doubt, so you can create what you want.

Before I started my business, I remember looking at high achievers and assumed they couldn't possibly have the kind of worry, self-doubt and frustration that I had. Once I started to coach those people, I realized that this was just not true. The self-sabotage triggers seem to happen to almost everyone.

The difference with high achievers is that they seek the help they need to transform those triggers. They know that self-doubt is going to be there, and they also know it's a choice about whether to support it or not. Unfortunately, the vast majority of people don't realize they have this choice, so they continually let it undermine them. They keep thinking negative thoughts based on their past programming, which leads to experiencing negative feelings, which reinforce the same neural pathways, which produce the neuro-chemicals that become addictive. In other words, they emotionally condition themselves to create more of their past.

Let's say you have a problem in your life, and you feel frustrated, and you blame it on someone else or on an external event. "My spouse is holding me back." "There's too much competition in my niche."

In essence, what you are saying is that this person is controlling how you think and feel, or that circumstances are responsible for your life. This means you're a victim to all that. Those thoughts bring a feeling of hopelessness, fear, anger and frustration. This can lead to inaction, where you give up on your goals. Alternatively, this can lead to actions such as leaving the relationship or changing the niche. Sometimes those decisions can be fruitful, but not if you're taking those actions from a disempowering place.

I CAN'T LET THIS NEGATIVE FEELING GO

Many people say, "I get what you're saying, but I can't seem to stop this negative feeling." That usually means they're addicted to the chemical reaction of that emotion. Remember, an addiction is something you think you can't stop. I know people who stay stuck in those emotions for years on end. Those emotions ruin their life, and they feel helpless.

The harsh truth is that they're in a relationship with those negative emotions. When I say to them, "Why are you so unhappy, why are you so bitter, why are you so angry?" They'll say, "I had this thing that happened to me years ago." It's like an identity that they are attached to. Who would they be without this event that shaped who they are today?

Often the current problems in a person's life have been created by their interpretation of that past event and the emotional conditioning it created. Letting go requires giving up your past and walking into the unknown.

RAISE YOUR CONSCIOUSNESS

In order for you to resolve the present challenges in your life, Einstein said you have to go to a greater level of belief than the original beliefs that created it. In other words, it's a combination of more empowering thoughts, meanings, feelings and actions that create the new level of consciousness and belief. Once conditioned into your subconscious, this becomes your new default way of operating.

BELIEVE YOU ALREADY HAVE IT

The most important thing, when it comes to achieving your goal, is to become a person that believes you already have it. That's what professional athletes do who work with performance coaches. They practice the thoughts and feel the feelings of playing their best, BEFORE they get out on the field. It's called 'mental rehearsal', which we'll talk about in more detail in a later chapter.

Believing you already have something is the secret to the Universe.

This is not a play on words. Just to make an important distinction, it's not about believing you will achieve your goal in the future – it's about believing you already RECEIVED IT. When you believe you've already received it, you become completely detached from the worry, desperation and anxiety that most people normally have around achieving important goals.

This is the energy that attracts your goal towards you.

In contrast, if you're constantly worried, you're sending a message to your unconscious that you don't deserve to have the goal. Your unconscious passes the message onto the Quantum Field. The Quantum Field is a theory about a plane of existence where thoughts manifest into reality. It's like the invisible code on a website that creates the images, videos, text, shapes and colors that you see.

When you broadcast worry to the Quantum Field, your goal will not only elude you; if you worry hard enough the field will give you more of what you don't want. This is because you are emotionally imprinting what you don't want. In other words, if you worry about lack of money, you're telling the Quantum Field to create a lack of money in your life.

The most important piece of the formula is to practice believing you ALREADY received the money you want. Imagine how you would think, feel and act as if you already had it – especially when times are toughest. By doing this, you are training your mind to experience the end product of future experiences today. The best way to predict your future is to create it and practice experiencing it ahead of time.

THE VIBRATION OF APPRECIATION

When you do achieve your goal, you must truly appreciate it and acknowledge where it came from. Most people make the mistake of achieving it and immediately moving onto the next goal without truly enjoying their success. This is why so many people reach the top and don't like the view. They haven't learned to integrate their wins and respect what they have been given. They fail to immerse themselves fully in the gratitude of their good fortune. It's about recognizing the interaction with the Quantum Field. When the Universe has given you exactly what you asked for, please pause and take note of that. The vibrational frequency of appreciation creates more of what you want. In other words, what you appreciate, appreciates. You are developing a relationship with the Quantum Field and because of this, it will give you even more great things. If you don't appreciate it, then the manifestation of your goal will depreciate and fade away. Does that make sense?

THE "HOW" DOSEN'T MATTER

If you know how to do something, it's not a big enough goal. It doesn't challenge you enough. This is why the 'how' always interferes with you believing without doubt. Even if you have a clear path to how, it probably won't work on the first attempt. If it's a big enough goal that's worthy of achieving, it's going to require some failure and course correction several times over. All great successes are built on a string of failures.

When you think about committing to an important goal, you have to keep envisioning it when all the evidence points to the contrary.

- *When people tell you that it's impossible.*
- *When you don't know how.*
- *When you're feeling not good enough.*
- *When you're not feeling capable enough.*
- *When you feel like you don't have the time.*
- *When you think you don't have the money.*
- *When there's too much competition.*

… that's when most of us stop believing. That's when you need to CREATE THE BELIEF again and again.

THE MOST IMPORTANT TIME TO BELIEVE IS WHEN THERE'S NO EVIDENCE OF YOUR VISION

Are you willing to believe in something when all the evidence is to the contrary?

When giving up seems like the best option?

When you fall down in the middle of the journey and it seems like everybody is passing you and doing so much better than you, that's when you need to believe in yourself the most.

We see this all the time with our clients here in MIC and particularly with our Certification Students at MindStory Academy. Sometimes they borrow our belief in them, which is an important first step. We believe in them 100%, because it's part of the jumpstarting process. There's never a doubt in our mind that they can achieve what they want to achieve. They wouldn't come to us with a dream unless, at some level, they believed in themselves. We are there to fan the flames of that belief until it turns into a burning desire.

BELIEVING WITHOUT DOUBT IS A CHOICE

When I first wanted to become a speaker and a coach, I had a lot of inner doubt about whether I could do it or not. This was based on my past experiences. As you know, I had a fear of public speaking and I was the worst salesperson in my company.

I turned it all around by learning to believe without self-doubt at progressively higher levels. This was a choice that I decided to make over and over again. Just like self-doubt is a choice that we make over and over again. This strengthens the neural pathways. Remember, the brain likes to be efficient. If self-doubt is the strongest neural circuit, the energy of the brain will go in that direction. If self-belief is the strongest circuit, the energy of the brain will go in that direction instead. It's just that simple. It's a pity this isn't taught in our school system.

As my level of believing in myself and my abilities without inner doubt continued to increase, so too did the results in my life. When I left my job as the No.1 salesperson in my company to pursue my dream of running my own business and becoming a world class speaker and coach, I had to practice believing without doubt at a whole new level.

What I loved doing was infusing that same level of belief into others and that's why I wanted to build my coaching and speaking business. When I was starting out, I didn't know how, but I believed that it was possible and I believed that it was the purpose of my life. I had to reinforce that belief over and over again.

That meant practicing living in the identity of someone who had a 7-figure speaking & coaching business. I was thinking, feeling and believing this way before I had ever achieved it. Eventually it became a reality.

That's what we're inviting you to do. We're inviting you to believe in something that maybe isn't reasonable, that maybe seems impossible at this time for you, that maybe there is no evidence for, that maybe nobody else believes in. It may feel scary to put yourself out there because what if you fail?

But what if you succeed? How committed are you to believing without doubt? How deeply are you willing to believe in your dreams?

YOUR RESULTS REFLECT YOUR DEEPEST BELIEFS

Consider the idea that your life is the feedback of what you actually believe. In other words, the level of success and fulfilment in the important areas of your life, are a direct reflection of what you believe in your heart. The stronger you believe in your success, the less you have to struggle to get there. Most people believe sometimes, then doubt, then go back to belief. This is called being double-minded. Imagine the Quantum Field is like a replicator on a Star Trek vessel, and it's like telling the replicator you want a successful business, so it goes to work creating it. Then the doubts says "but I don't deserve it," so the replicator stops creating it.

The more you believe in a consistent way, the message to the Quantum Field is clear and it can do its work. It's replicating, and you're just waiting for it to manifest into this reality. It's in the mail, they've already shipped it, you're just waiting for it to arrive. Whether it's regular mail or express delivery depends on your level of believing without doubt.

This is simply the mechanics. It's the commitment to believing your goal has already happened before it has, without any doubt messing up the processing cycle. We want you to practice believing in the thing you want without any shred of doubt. It takes practice. You have to teach your mind that this is your reality now.

HOMEPLAY

CLOSED EYE PROCESS

Here is a short exercise to practice believing without self-doubt.

STEP 1 - Close your eyes and relax for a few minutes. Hold your head in a comfortable position and let go of any tension in the shoulders. Let your back support you. Imagine that a golden thread runs vertically up through your spine and straight up into the sky – and imagine that this thread supports you. Let yourself relax, safely held by that thread. This relaxed upright stance is the natural position of belief, and it will soon be as natural to you as breathing.

STEP 2 - Now remember a time when you believed in something without any inner doubt. You had unshakeable belief. Return fully to that time now, seeing through your own eyes, hearing the sounds of being right there and feeling how great you felt.

STEP 3 - Now make the colors brighter and richer, the sounds louder and allow your feelings of unshakeable belief to intensify.

STEP 4 - Notice the location where the feeling of unshakeable belief is strongest in your body. Give this feeling of unshakeable belief a color, and move that color up to the top of your head and have it flow down to the tips of your toes. Double the level of brightness. Double it again!

STEP 5 - Think of a big goal you want to achieve. What would you believe differently? How would you act differently? How would you make decisions differently after you've achieved this goal?

STEP 6 - Next, vividly imagine that your goal has already happened. You have received it. What are the 3 feelings you're most experiencing? What does your life look like? What are you saying inside your own mind as you achieved this goal?

STEP 7 - Now, identify a next action step you can take immediately towards achieving this result and visualize yourself effortlessly taking that action while believing without self-doubt.

THE POWER OF 3

Sometimes it's hard to adopt a new belief so if you can list 3 beliefs, 2 of which are already true now, then your mind is more likely to accept the 3rd as being also true. It helps the mind open to new possibilities.

For example, say you want to believe that you're capable of building a successful consulting business.

FACT #1 - I've got a degree in Human Resources.

FACT #2 - I've spent 11 years employed in Human Resources.

NEW BELIEF - I've got what it takes to be an HR consultant.

Section 2

VISION

VISION

In this section, we'll explore the different aspects of Vision. This is Part 2 of the AVARA Coaching Model. It's about identifying a negative overarching vision that might be lurking in your subconscious mind. Then, it's about creating a more empowering overarching vision.

You can start at Vision in the model especially if you have some form of CONFUSION going on. For example, an inner conflict, uncertainty about how to proceed, indecision or feeling overwhelmed. You might hear yourself say something like:

"I feel like I'm spinning my wheels."
"I am overwhelmed and working hard but
still don't seem to get anywhere."
"I can't decide where to focus."

Try using the model on your own area of CONFUSION.

Step A – Issue: What's a problem in your life? Describe the situation. No editing. We'll refer to this as your Limiting MindStory.

E.g. I'm procrastinating about booking myself to speak at events, because I doubt I can do a good job anymore. I started on the speaking circuit and got good reviews. Then, I got booked at a big, high profile event. I got mostly negative feedback. They said I wasn't at the same level as the speakers they normally book. I got very discouraged and full of self-doubt after that.

Step B - Facts: Now see if you can state what you wrote above as objectively as possible. That means to separate facts from your interpretation, no adjectives, adverbs or descriptive phrases. Just the issue without your feelings or thoughts about it. From an outside perspective what would everyone agree on?

E.g. I got feedback at a speaking engagement. I haven't booked anymore engagements.

Step C – Limiting Version	Step D – Empowering Version
Now, you're going to break your MindStory down into its components parts here in the "Limiting Story" section. Then, we'll transform it in the "Empowering Story" section in the right-hand column. Start by going down this left column first, then go onto Step D, in the right-hand column.	Now that you've broken your MindStory down into its components parts, we'll transform it in this "Empowering Story". Look at what you wrote in each of the parts in the left column, and create a positive version here.
1) Acceptance: What are the limiting feelings, thoughts and meaning you are giving to the situation? Express it like this *I am* (negative feeling) *because* (negative thought). *I'm making this situation mean...* (your interpretation). *E.g. **I'm feeling** humiliated **because** I got bad reviews. **I'm making this mean** that I'm a bad speaker and always will be, I'm not very professional, I'm not meant to be out there speaking.*	**1) Acceptance**: What are more empowering feelings, thoughts and meanings you could give to the situation? Express it like this *I have chosen to be* (positive feeling) *because* (positive thought). *A better meaning I could give this situation is...* *E.g. **I have chosen to be** compassionate with myself and willing to learn from the situation because I'm new to big audiences. **A better meaning is** that it's normal to have a challenging situation from time to time. I could have given myself more prep time. I could learn to get better as a speaker for these kinds of high stakes events.*

I AM FEELING	I HAVE CHOSEN TO BE
BECAUSE	**BECAUSE**
I'M MAKING THIS MEAN (List all, even if they seem unlikely or silly)	*A BETTER MEANING (that would feel empowering to you)*

2) Vision: What is your possible future a YEAR FROM NOW if you live from this limiting MindStory? Be specific.

E.g. I won't be able to grow my business through speaking. I'll have to give up on my long-time dream of speaking on big stages.

2) Vision: What is your possible future a YEAR FROM NOW if you live from this more empowering MindStory? Be specific.

E.g. I'm living my dream of speaking on big stages. I've just received another $10,000 fee for a speaking engagement.

3) **Action:** What action or inaction is taking place? *E.g. I'm avoiding making any calls to meeting planners about potentially speaking at their event.*	3) **Action:** What actions could you take to achieve this empowering VISION? Anything goes. No editing. List at least 7 ideas. Then choose 1 idea and break it down to specific, small next steps in Step E below. *E.g. Get a mentor* 1. 2. 3. 4. 5. 6. 7.
4) **Reprogram:** What is a recent event or experience that triggered this issue? Use present tense as if you were there now. *E.g. I'm at a speaking engagement and the tech isn't working properly. It's really throwing me off. I'm also very nervous because I've never spoken in front of such a huge audience. I left my preparation until the very last minute, so that's made me feel less confident. I can tell the audience isn't engaging with me. I feel guilty and embarrassed by the bad reviews.*	4) **Reprogram:** What is a similar event or experience that might happen in the near future where it's playing out in a more empowering way? Use present tense as if you were there now. *E.g. I am at a big speaking engagement and the tech is working well. I am confident about how to engage a big audience. I have properly prepared and I'm feeling good about myself and my material. I'm getting great reviews. I feel proud of myself.*

5) Attention: What are the limiting beliefs here or negative Self Talk? List all, even if they seem mean-spirited, unlikely or silly. *E.g. I'm such an amateur! I don't have what it takes to do this. People don't like me or my material. What was I thinking, trying to speak at that event?*	**5) Attention**: What might be your new beliefs or Self Talk from this more empowering MindStory? Start your sentence with this progressive affirmation: "Every day in every way I'm ..." *E.g. Every day in every way I'm becoming a better and more confident speaker.*

Step E - Specific Next Actions: Pick one idea from your empowering ACTION section above. What are 1 to 3 specific, small, next steps to get that started? Give each a date, delegate where possible. By breaking down big goals into small steps, it makes them feel easier to accomplish.

#	Action	Who	When
Eg	*Call my speaker colleague to see if he'll mentor me*	*Me*	*Monday*
1.			
2.			
3.			

CHAPTER 4

The Magic of Thinking BIG

DAVE'S STORY

Here's an example of how I came to live my vision, as you might relate to it. You'll recall I went from zero to hero in sales and completely turned my life around. For the next 7 years, I went from strength to strength. I loved what I did with a passion. But alas, all good things must come to an end, and it was time for the next chapter of my life. For as long as I could remember, I had a vision of running my own business, being a world-class speaker and coaching others develop their mindset. I wanted to help people design their own lives.

That's when I started out on the next phase of my hero's journey. I felt both relieved and terrified at the same time. The next six months were the most difficult time I ever faced in my life. I had taken a huge leap of faith, but the future was highly uncertain. After all, I had left the security of my job. I retreated into myself, and I watched as my savings dwindled away and I maxed out my credit cards. I had no clear direction. I was starting from scratch all over again. I felt lost. Night after night, I did a lot of soul-searching. Every time I thought about my old life, I longed to return to the safety and security of that comfort zone. But deep down, I knew I had it in me to get out there and be successful as a speaker and coach. How could I get started? Many times, I wanted to give up.

Then, one day, something extraordinary happened. I was standing in the driveway where I was living. I had an awakening, a download of sorts. I heard a voice deep within me say:

I'm not sure why I'm in this dark place, but one thing I know for sure, is that everything happens for a reason. Great good will come from this. I made the right choice. The struggle is part of the journey. I'm going to figure this out. I'm going to bounce back bigger and better than ever. The best has yet to come for me. It's only a matter of time.

The moment I made what seemed to be a declaration, all worry, fear and anxiety about my future vanished completely. I felt what I can only describe as a clear space all around me. I knew for certain that I was going to be okay. I kept bringing up my vision and immersing myself in the end outcome as if it had already happened over and over again.

I asked myself, "How would I feel if I was living this vision?"

"I would feel happy, grateful, secure, fulfilled. I would feel joyful, excited, inspired, peaceful."

I deliberately practiced feeling those feelings every day. Then, out of nowhere, I got a phone call that changed my life forever. I'll get back to what happened a bit later.

ACHIEVING YOUR VISION IS PREDICTABLE

Achieving your goals and vision is not something that just 'happens' to some people and not to others. It's a predictable process that has a structure and sequence. You create your vision by forming new habits of thinking, feeling and taking action – as we've already been sharing with you in this book.

We believe that anybody who says that success is just about luck – is wrong. You contribute greatly to the process. Yes, there are many ingredients. But you can stack the odds in your favor significantly.

An inner transformation like what happened to me can happen for you too. Our understanding of how the brain and mind works has evolved exponentially over the last few decades. For example, things like phobias that used to take years to clear up can now be cleared up in a few minutes. Most people can think of a time when their lives changed in just a few moments. Perhaps it was meeting a certain type of person or receiving information that you'd heard many times before but which suddenly clicked when presented in a different way.

It doesn't have to take a long time for change to occur – but you still have to be patient and know that once you are consistently moving forward in the direction of your dreams, then positive change and transformation are inevitable.

WHY CHANGE IS HARD

Raising the bar and deciding to think bigger can be challenging. Trying to take control of your thoughts and feelings takes a whole other skill set that you may not have been practicing before. The reason we don't immediately embrace an exciting vision and turn into better versions of ourselves is because change is hard. The "Unwillingness Trigger" kicks in, which makes us not want to do hard things.

The fact is, change is uncomfortable and many people have been conditioned to dislike being uncomfortable. What's the point of being uncomfortable when you can just stay comfortable? But then you stagnate. The fear of discomfort often overshadows the dislike of being stagnant and feeling stuck.

Whether you're trying to grow your business, or you're trying to lose weight, or trying to increase sales, or you're trying just to get your first client or recruit your first prospect - no matter what it is, if it's different than what you have been used to, it's going to feel hard.

I remind myself that change is hard on purpose. Just like our fitness workouts are hard on purpose because they make us stronger.

High achievers find a way of being okay with discomfort. It actually becomes an enjoyable part of life. When they want to go to the next level of success, they know they've got to put new habits in place, to think better thoughts, to feel better feelings and take more consistent action.

THE POWER OF HABITUALIZED ACTIONS

The actions that create the most results are the habitual ones. Those positive and negative things that you do without thinking about it. The ones on automatic pilot. The key is to create empowering habits in your life. These will override the negative habits and will propel you massively forward.

Every thought you think fires up a set of circuits in the brain, which releases a chemical reaction so that you feel exactly the way you are thinking. This means that a thought of unworthiness will produce a feeling of shame. This also means that a thought of worthiness will produce a feeling of confidence.

If you have reinforced unworthiness over many years, that's not going to change overnight. Behavioral scientists tell us that it takes between 21 and 66 days to form lasting habits. That's why a big focus at MindStory Academy is to support you to rebuild the muscles of confidence, certainty, belief, clarity, gratitude, and all the MindStories that help you stay positive, energized and successful.

THE POWER OF VISION

The power of vision is one of the most important things we'd love you to take away from this book. Most people have a hazy vision or no vision at all. They just take what life brings them. A self-created vision is the fuel that makes your goals rush towards you. Imprinting a compelling, long-term vision in your subconscious mind will then work away constantly in the background, driving and propelling you towards your ultimate destination. The quality of your vision is everything. In this dark period of world history, more than ever, we need to arm ourselves with a crystal clear, invincible vision. In fact, the more people who create a compelling vision, not just for themselves but for a better world… this what will turn things around. We can't keep waiting for someone else to do it for us.

The people we have worked with, who have enjoyed the greatest successes, came to us with vague goals, such as 'I'd like to make more money' or 'I'd like to be successful.' Together, however, we helped them refine those goals into a crystal clear, end outcome, that they were truly passionate about. Only then were they able to access their creative power to bring about the results they wanted.

THINKING SMALL IS A RECIPE FOR FAILURE

How you think and feel decides whether you succeed or fail because it controls the release of your power. Most people think way too small and therefore lack excitement and feel unmotivated to achieve their goals. Consequently, their goals never reach their unconscious mind. It's not because they aim too high and miss; it's because they aim too low, and score.

High achievers, on the other hand, continuously experience massive releases of their power, because the goals that they want are reaching their unconscious unhindered by self-sabotage. That's when the magic happens.

Showing yourself what you're capable of is the biggest thrill in the world.

The reason why we recommend that you embrace discomfort and growth and see what you can do in this world is because it's so much more fun than being comfortable and watching life pass you by.

Think of an area of life where you're okay getting uncomfortable. For me, it was working out in the gym. I knew that if I wanted stronger muscles, I needed to lift heavier weights. I was able to transfer that willingness when I wanted to start an online business back in 2009. It looked daunting, all the things I'd have to learn, all the mistakes I'd have to make before I got there. But at that point, I'd learned to look forward to the discomfort of hard things. I knew to focus on what was on the other side of it, the joy of the end goal. By practicing that over and over again, I learned to associate difficult tasks with feelings of joy.

HOMEPLAY

Here are some exercises to build an invincible vision. Visioning takes careful planning and constant reinforcement, along with course correction and being willing to learn from mistakes. Most people set goals and tend to forget about them. They get distracted, lose their vision, and then just settle for what life brings. They never understand how to use the power of an invincible vision.

WHERE DO YOU WANT TO BE IN 5 YEARS?

This process is designed to activate another part of your brain, and so the best way to do it is to not edit yourself at all. Anything goes. You don't have to act on anything you write down here; it's just about exploration at this stage.

Answer these questions as if you had no obstacles; as if there were no money issues, no time issues, no issues around your age, your health, your abilities, and especially no issues about what other people might think about or expect from you.

If there were no obstacles...

- what do you really want that you don't have in your life now?
- what would make you most happy?
- what way of being are you most eager to cultivate?
- what would you most like to do with the remainder of your life?
- how do you most want to contribute?

5-YEAR VISION

Write down the exact date five years ago:

What were you doing this time five years ago?

What goals did you want to achieve?

Did you manage to achieve them or was it hit and miss?

Answer these questions quickly, going from your gut...

1. What type of environment would you most excel in?

2. What type of home would you like to live in?

3. What kind of car would you like to be driving?

4. How much time off would you like every week and every year?

5. How much time would you like to spend traveling around the world?

6. How much time do you want to spend with your family?

YOUR VISION STATEMENT

Try writing out a paragraph listing what's important to you. Elements to include are:

Destiny: Tap into what you FEEL you are meant to be doing with your life.

Mission: Include the path you take to get there and the specific means by which you can accomplish that vision. It is comprised of who you are going to be and what you are going to do to reach your vision.

Values: Write down your three most important values that you wish to live by. Include words such as "joy" or "gratitude" or "wellness" or "creativity" that help you keep true to your path and to yourself. These words will help you be more aligned with your ethics and what is most important to cultivate in your life.

> **Remember a vision is a preview of your future life. Don't leave it to chance and settle for whatever fate throws at you. Take control right now and create your vision.**

Here are two examples. One from Dave. One from Carla. Below that, write out your own version.

EXAMPLE OF DAVE'S VISION

I'm so happy and grateful that I am happy, healthy, vibrant and energetic – living the life of my dreams. I am travelling the world, staying in the most wonderful locations while doing the work I love with a passion – helping people with their mindset.

I'm speaking to large audiences everywhere, training them to upgrade their mindset and believe without doubt, so they can live their ultimate lifestyle. I have attracted the perfect business and personal relationships based on trust.

I hear from hundreds of people every day who tell me how much my products, trainings and seminars are enhancing the quality of their lives. It all feels so fulfilling.

And, even though I'm financially free, and a great example of a fabulous life, what I'm most proud of is who I have grown into. I refused to compromise on my dream and I stayed true to my deepest values.

I feel an immense sense of purpose, joy and gratitude every day – that I'm doing exactly what I'm destined to do.

EXAMPLE OF CARLA'S VISION

I'm so happy and grateful that I am in the flow, creatively inspired, healthy, and vibrant – living life on my own terms. I am helping people free their minds, feel more empowered and on purpose.

I'm speaking, coaching, training, facilitating and writing for audiences around the world. I have the ideal business and personal relationships based on trust and mutual respect.

I know in my heart that my offerings are making a huge difference for the right people. I am enjoying the journey and am financially free, living a lifestyle that works for me. I'm living my values and growing spiritually every day.

I feel an immense sense of purpose, joy, gratitude and right action every day – that I'm doing exactly what I'm destined to do, with the help of seen and unseen benevolent guidance.

MY 5-YEAR VISION

It is now _____ (date 5 years from now)

I'm so happy and grateful that I...

_____

_____

_____

_____

_____

_____

_____

_____

_____

_____

_____

_____

_____

_____

## CHAPTER 5

Get Clarity on How to Serve

Nobody cares how much you know – until they know how much you care.
— Theodore Roosevelt

CARLA'S STORY

Here's an example of how I came to find my vision by realizing there were certain types of people I'm meant to serve. It might give you some ideas about how it could play out for you. I had a vague vision. I wanted to help empower people in some way. I had no idea how I wanted to empower them, or how I would make a living doing that. I studied all kinds of personal development through my teens and early twenties. Then I studied public speaking and acting to get over my shyness. Amazingly, I got a job that involved public speaking to thousands of new college students. I ran them through icebreaker games so they wouldn't feel as lonely on campus.

A few years later, in my late twenties, I decided to start my own business. I joined a business incubator for people under 30 years old. It was excellent in terms of giving me entrepreneurial skills, but something was "off" for me. My mentors kept saying you have to work really hard and stop wasting your time having fun. Many of the twentysomethings were clearly more into partying than staying focused on building a business. I got that, but I also didn't want to "throw the baby out with the bathwater." I felt people DID need fun to balance all the work. I grew up in a family where everyone worked really hard and never had any fun, and there was a big price to pay. Those were the kinds of people I wanted to help.

My family was composed of serious, solemn, linear, logical, academic, achievement-oriented people who were immigrants to Canada. My mother was British and my father was from Slovakia. They didn't value fun, playfulness and humor. I remember the following incident as a kid when I was 10 years old. We were around the dinner table. I heard something at school, so I said:

> "Mom, why don't cannibals like to eat clowns?
> "I don't know, dear, why?"
> "Because they taste funny."
> "That doesn't make any sense, dear. Clowns don't normally frequent the jungles of Africa where cannibals can be found. Just be quiet and eat your beans."

I grew up, and I followed in her footsteps. I became serious, goal oriented, academic and diligent. I worried most of the time about reaching my goals. I did seven years of post-secondary education, with three part-time jobs all the way through. Remember when my public speaking teacher told me I should lighten up? That made me do a complete right turn in my life.

Suffice it to say, I chose to focus on fun as a teambuilding tool for workplaces. It was the idea of balancing work and play. I didn't think being overly serious about everything was a good idea for me, or for anyone. There were statistics that groups that play together, stay together. A fun work environment meant less conflict, less absenteeism, more motivation, higher sales, and staying healthier.

Some teams naturally had that sense of joy and camaraderie, but some didn't. They needed help to break free of a constant pattern of stress and negativity. It was hard at first trying to sell the idea of helping people be more productive as a team, by getting them to play together. Most managers and business owners felt sure that would lead to LESS productivity. The amount of rejection I received led to me losing my motivation for doing this business. I looked at my cash flow and decided I'd better go get a job. I had only one booking coming up.

My last booking was to work with a team in Savannah, Georgia. After an afternoon of working and playing with her team, the organizer, Mary Beth Wilson, invited me out for dinner. In her glorious southern accent, she said, "That was just wonderful. It's exactly what we needed to come together." I felt so glad to hear that.

At the time, I never thought to include a personal story or talk about my mission, vision or purpose for doing this kind of work. Mostly, that was because I wasn't clear. That dinner with Mary Beth changed everything because she asked me, *"What got you into this line of work? What is your WHY?"*

I did explain about coming from a family that was all work and no play, but as the evening wore on, I realized there was a deeper reason that I'd forgotten about. It was about my mother. You know, the one who didn't get the clown joke? At first, I was uncomfortable about sharing that story with Mary Beth, because I felt vulnerable about how personal it was. Yet, the Mint Juleps we were drinking started to kick in.

I told her that I had just remembered a deeper "why". It had to do with mother. She was an amazing social change leader, but she really was all work and no play. Then, she got cancer when I was still in my 20's. In fact she was diagnosed with not one but two kinds of cancer, both with a dim prognosis. So, the notion that life is short became very real to her, as well as to me.

The irony was that her entire personality changed. She said, *"Let's have fun!"* I'd never known what fun meant to her but I soon found out. It started with writing poetry, wearing wild clothes, and clipping flowers in her hair. Then, she started singing and doing interpretive dance and all this expressive stuff—not caring what people thought anymore.

She loved being with people who made her laugh. And, I'd never seen my mother laugh – you know the big, hearty belly kind of laugh – until she was very ill. She really just let it all go. She didn't care if the chequebook balanced. She didn't care if there were wrinkles in the tablecloth. She said, "I just want to LIVE as best I can right now!"

During all this she warned me not to go down the same road as she had— not to be overly serious, worried, frustrated and pushing at the expense of everything else.

In fact, I remember her saying just a few months before she passed, "You don't know when your last day will be. For me, I know it's coming soon. But you don't know – maybe today is your last day. Do you really want to spend it rushing around trying to fit in one more thing until you feel exhausted? I lived my whole life like that and what did it get me? Will anyone remember me at my funeral for all the things I got done on my task list? I think not."

It's like she was now living the way she wished she lived her whole life. And she was giving me a chance to start young instead of waiting until the end like she did. So I made that promise to my mother on her deathbed, that I would lighten up and love the moments, and I took it a step further and decided to lighten up the world.

Now, whenever I think of her, she is smiling and laughing like she was at the end. Although when I look at old photos, she is almost never smiling. But I can remember the person that she became at the end of her life.

I was telling Mary Beth all that, and she said to me, "That's important. You have to tell that story." So I did and it changed the game for me. As soon as I started telling that story it went in deeper as my personal WHY. It kept reminding me of my deeper purpose and so it quadrupled my resilience and also seemed to be very helpful for those who heard it…inspiring them to find their deeper purpose for their life and work.

This quote by Ursula Le Guin, science-fiction author, became my value system to live by: *It's good to have an end to journey towards but it's the journey that matters in the end.*

After that, I decided NOT to quit my business, but to quadruple my commitment. True to that number, I quadrupled my business income within six months, and I never looked back.

WE ALL LOSE OUR MOTIVATION AT TIMES

We all go through periods of life when we lose our motivation. It can be a lost or lethargic feeling where you are just going through the motions, but you feel a general disinterest in life. If that's ever happened, or is happening now, it might mean that you need to reinvent yourself and get more clarity on a new vision and direction for life.

According to the US Department of Labor, some of the careers that are most in demand today didn't even exist six years ago. People now change their careers at least six times in their lifetime, their long-term relationships at least three times, and their homes at least twelve times.

In short, people are reinventing themselves at a rate never seen before in recorded history. What exists now is a whole lot of people going through constant reinvention and feeling entirely challenged about how they can deal with it.

It can feel uncomfortable when you're between two worlds. The old way hasn't quite disappeared, but you feel its relevance in your life is fading away. At the same time, the next phase of life hasn't yet appeared on the horizon. It's a kind of barren place we call the *Winter of Change*. It's also known as "the void" or "the abyss" or to quote a popular cartoon, "I know that when one door closes, another always opens, but, man, those hallways are a bitch!"

HOW TO BREAK FREE FROM "THE WINTER OF CHANGE"

After years of studying personal development and "success" tools, it's easy to believe that being in 'The Winter of Change' is somehow wrong. There seems to be an underlying belief that you have to be positive and productive all the time. If you aren't, you've somehow fallen under the clutches of self-sabotage again.

In some cases, that's true, and in other cases it's just the natural ebb and flow of life. Just like in the cycles of nature, your creative life force energy needs time to rest. The Winter of Change means that the last harvest is gone and the soil needs time to replenish itself.

The Winter of Change is a very important part of your reinvention process and to try to push it away, ignore it or anesthetize it, can actually mean you miss out on the next harvest of your life.

That's the time when people are most likely to feel lost, lethargic, confused and unclear about what's next. Things can feel meaningless. Things you used to enjoy can feel pointless. Those are totally normal experiences to be having.

The Winter of Change is often the time people are least likely to ask for help and the time they most need it. This book is designed to help you during the Winter of Change, so you go through it with ease and grace, and actually enjoy it. People go through reinventions at different times of their life and in different areas of life – health, relationships, career, finances, personal development, etc.

For example, a common time for people to enter the Winter of Change is right after retirement. Even if you've been looking forward to retirement, it can feel strange and barren once you're there. Another time is right after your kids leave home, even though you've been looking forward to having all this time for yourself, it can feel lonely. Even more surprisingly, another such time is after you just finished an incredible career accomplishment.

ACHIEVING A BIG GOAL CAN TRIGGER DESPAIR

In fact, five years into my business, that happened to me. I had a clear vision of where I wanted to be in five years, and I went there. I was going across the continent speaking at all these huge events, getting standing ovations and staying in five-star hotels. It was exactly what I'd envisioned when I first started out. Then, I remember I came back to my hotel room after having spoken at a hugely successful event. It was literally five years since I'd created that vision. I'd done it! However, instead of feeling elated, I actually felt lost. I couldn't figure it out.

It actually marked the beginning of a two-year Winter of Change for me. I no longer wanted to keep doing this career. It didn't feel meaningful to me anymore. Yet, I didn't know what else to do. It was a frightening time for me. That's when I learned that people cyclically go through these barren Winter of Change periods in their lives. Often, when you achieve a vision, your entire life force energy can come to a screeching halt. Done that, now what?

So often, people feel frustrated that their dreams always seem beyond their reach, but once you reach them, it can feel empty. At that point, you will need to rest, replenish and give yourself the space to create a whole other new journey to go on.

Eventually I learned to embrace this period of time instead of resisting it. I let myself totally replenish my creative coffers. After five years of focused effort on that one goal, I needed a rest. Even though it seemed worrisome in terms of losing momentum and financial security, I knew in my heart that it was the right thing to do. Ironically, that change of heart helped me move through the Winter of Change far more quickly. Not only did I need to replenish, but I also needed to let go of my old identity, go into the abyss and let it all fall away. Then, just when I thought nothing new would start to happen in my life, the Spring of Change began to bloom.

WHAT IS THE "SPRING OF CHANGE"?

The 'Spring of Change' is when the new ideas start to blossom and your energy and motivation starts to come back. It became clear that I didn't actually need to do anything different in terms of my core offerings as a communication, performance and leadership expert. HOW I was doing my career needed to change. I'd been working seven days a week, accepting every contract, for fear of not having enough income. I'd been living from a place of scarcity about income, and worried I'd be labeled as an imposter. The dreaded 'Imposter Syndrome' seems to be very common with experts in their field. There's always this little voice of doubt that says, "What do you have to share that people want to hear?"

It takes courage to release the old, the familiar and what seems secure, but the truth is there isn't any security in things that don't have meaning for you anymore. It's actually in the movement towards the new and the adventurous, where you get your vitality back and you get your life back. That's where the real security is.

HOW TO CHANGE A CORE MINDSTORY

I became clear on the old MindStory "archetype" that needed replacing – The Imposter. Then, I learned to embody a more empowering MindStory, which I labeled The Expert. As we said, a MindStory is a patterned way of being that shows up in the human condition, in stories, myths and culture. Stories are how the brain organizes beliefs, thoughts, feelings, expectations, roles, etc. We download these patterns subconsciously and then the MindStories go on autopilot, running our lives for good or for bad indefinitely unless we change them.

I also had a MindStory script I'll call "Scarcity" that I needed to delete and replace with a MindStory script called "Prosperity." I grew up believing such phrases as:

"You have to work very hard for money."
"Money is the root of all evil."
"Having money means someone else loses money."
"If you have money, you become a target."

As such, I often felt uncomfortable having too much money, and anytime I did get some, I'd spend it very quickly. That meant I usually felt this pressure to work hard, not feeling like I had enough.

I came to realize that money was not the problem; it was just a form of energy exchange. It's what you *interpret* about money that makes it a problem. In fact, from many perspectives you could argue that poverty is the root of all evil. It causes untold suffering all over the world. And logically, it doesn't make sense that if you have money, then someone else doesn't. There is not a finite sum of money in the world. Money is created from the value you provide, at least that's how it often is. There are exceptions, of course. In the end, however, I saw that what I thought, how I interpreted money in life, was hugely responsible for my financial situation. Worrying about having enough money was using my creative imagination to create that which I didn't want.

I began to imagine having the kind of money I wanted to have, feeling worthy of it, seeing myself do good things with it, providing excellent value for the money I received. By reinforcing those MindStories, my external reality around money began to match it. With that in place, I only took contracts that seemed right for me, rather than taking just anything.

To override the imposter syndrome, I needed to feel like I was providing top notch value. I decided to "up" my game. I worked with the best coaches and experts, I rewrote my materials, and I redid my marketing to reflect this higher quality of offering. That way, I felt comfortable charging more, and feeling worthy of reaching out to my ideal clients, instead of anyone who would hire me. Therefore, I ended up not having to work so much. More opportunities showed up without as much effort. I was making more, enjoying my work more, and leading a more balanced life. Once those new MindStories were in place, the Spring of Change came forth. My energy, creativity and motivation came back. It's like my soul felt safe moving forward again.

Reinvention takes place in our world frequently now; the habit of being able to reinvent yourself is an important tool for surviving and thriving .

HOMEPLAY

In this section, you can take steps to help you remember a hidden, deeper vision that can increase your motivation, or it can help you create a new and compelling vision for your life in order to move forward again. Remember: Don't keep the idea of reinvention as just an idea. Take action. Most people get stuck in the Winter of Change for much longer than necessary, because they don't do an exploration like this from time to time.

DISCOVERING YOUR PASSION WORKSHEET

This first process will help you discover what you are truly passionate about because passion is what you may be missing right now.

Passions are different than interests. Many people spend years dabbling in areas of interest without feeling truly fulfilled. Interests will only sustain you for so long, whereas passions can feed you for a lifetime.

There is a unique way we all belong to the world. Apprentice yourself to that discovery. — David Whyte

On the next page, you'll fill in the 3 columns:

Column 1
What is Unique about Me?

Make a list of all the things that are unique about you. These could be character strengths or even weaknesses. Ann McGee-Cooper was bad at time management and built an entire business based on her bestselling book *Time Management for Unmanageable People.*

Fill up the entire column. Examples of these could be:

Personality traits - Strengths or weaknesses. E.g. good at influencing people, excellent attention to detail, bad at time management.

Circumstances of your life - E.g. your cultural heritage, a disability, born into a family of gymnasts, one of 12 siblings.

Experiences you've had - E.g. 10 years in marketing at Dell, having lived on 4 continents, overcoming cancer, starting a foundation, meeting Nelson Mandela.

Column 2
What Have I Learned? What is My Expertise?

Make a list of things that you have learned. Fill up the entire column. These could be:

A Technical Expertise - E.g. health care management, spreadsheets, music composition, car repair, hair styling, architecture, teaching, blogging, MEd in Adult Education.

Things you've learned as a student of life - E.g. surviving a broken home, leading a balanced life, raising children, overcoming an addiction.

Column 3
What's Missing in the World?

Make a list of needs that aren't being met in the world. It could be for a small or a large portion of the population. These could be general or specific, small or large needs.

For example, what might seem missing for you is:

- better housing for seniors
- workplaces where people feel engaged
- people with savings for a rainy day
- attractive women's shoes in size 10 or higher
- online auctions for golf and scuba gear
- rooftop gardens in apartment buildings
- clean water for people in Southern India
- an app that connects digital nomads with housing around the world with home offices

DISCOVER YOUR PASSION WORKSHEET

After you've finished, circle the top 3 in each of these columns that have the most impact for you

What is Unique About Me?	What Have I Learned? What is My Experience?	What's Missing in the World?

FIND A HUNGRY AUDIENCE

The next exercise will help you find who to serve and how to serve them. This exercise takes about 10 minutes. You may already know this, but doing the exercise may surprise you.

TYPES OF COMMUNITIES I WANT TO WORK WITH (COLUMN 1)

Start by making a list of the types of individuals, groups or communities you want to work with. You can list them by:

- **The work they do** (e.g. industries, professions, trades, job titles, etc.).
- **Population segments** (e.g. GenX, women, retired people, teens, married people, parents, people who live in Seattle, etc.).
- **Non work-related groups** (e.g. French speaking people, the Jewish community, dog lovers, golf enthusiasts, joggers, antique car aficionados, ex-cons, gifted learners, university students, etc.).

Find a broad enough market that you have enough people in it, but not so broad that people view you as a generalist. It's harder to market yourself if you're too general. Many new business owners say they'll work with anyone, but think about that from the buyer's perspective. If you needed a liver transplant would you choose a surgeon who generalized or someone who was a liver transplant expert? People want to buy from someone who understands their specific problems and knows how to fix them.

Warning: make sure you choose a segment of the population you want to learn more about. I once made the mistake of creating a program on drug and alcohol awareness for junior high school students. In the first place, they were not interested in that topic. I changed my focus to comedy improvisation training, thinking a creative outlet would be a more positive way of keeping them from becoming substance abusers. It certainly helped. However, I found I didn't enjoy learning about or working with that segment of the population enough for me to continue. Sometimes it helps to offer your services on a volunteer basis for that community first, before investing too much time or money.

After you have made a list of communities, circle your top three in the first column.

WHAT HURTS? WHAT IS CHANGING? (COLUMN 2)

Keeping your three communities in mind, what hurts these people?
What problems do they face?
What bothers them the most?
You can go back to your list of what's missing in the world and see if there is any overlap.

For example, sales people really dislike cold calling. Pregnant women often have lower back problems. Newly sober people need supportive communities. Workplaces need to be more respectful of diversity, etc.

Another way to look at it is, "What is changing?" For example, the Baby Boomers are getting older and will need increasingly more health care. Salmon is becoming an endangered species, which is affecting the environment and the livelihood of fishermen. Due to many companies downsizing, there are more freelance consultants who need help setting up their own consulting business.

Make a list of everything you can think of. For example, if you chose dieticians, your list of what hurts or what is changing might look like this:

- Work/life balance
- Lack of follow-up by other team members
- Keeping up with technological changes
- Health care mergers and re-structuring
- Change in academic certification requirements
- Roles and responsibilities increasing without proper mentorship

- Dress code keeps changing
- Poor communication between people in different departments
- Downsizing and job loss
- Office politics

Once you have completed that list, circle your top three choices in the second column.

HOW CAN PEOPLE BENEFIT FROM MY PASSION/EXPERTISE? (COLUMN 3)

Finally, look at what benefits you can offer your chosen communities. Focus on solving their problems using your passion and expertise. See if you can write it in the form of an article title. For example, if you chose dieticians your list might look like this:

- How to create a culture of open communication in a health care setting
- The dietician's guide to navigating office politics
- How to survive and thrive as a dietician in the new economy

FIND WHO TO SERVE

Types of Communities I Want to Work With (Circle Your Top 3)	What Hurts? What's Changing for Them? (Circle Your Top 3)	How Specifically Can People Benefit from My Passion and Expertise?
Industries, professions, trades, job titles:	What hurts?	
Population Segments:		
	What's Changing for Them?	
Non work-related groups:		

YOUR EXPERTISE MISSION STATEMENT

Look again at the answers in your "Discover Your Passion" Worksheet and your "Find Who to Serve" Worksheet and combine your top items in all columns into this statement. This will summarize expertise to keep you focused.

It may require some playing around with the wording until you get a clear statement. Use this process to get started.

My passion is to use my _____
(Uniqueness – Passion Worksheet)

to help _____
(Type of community-Hungry Audience Worksheet)

deal with _____
(What hurts. What is changing. Passion Worksheet)

I will do this by _____
(How people can benefit – Hungry Audience Worksheet)

so that _____
(What's missing in the world – Passion Worksheet)

Examples:

My passion is to use my conflict resolution and mediation training
to help the hi tech industry
deal with interpersonal communication breakdowns.
I will do this by teaching them conflict resolution skills,
so that their work teams are more collaborative, creative and effective.

My passion is to use my research ability and experience with the Gallup organization
to help CEO's and business owners
deal with changes in the economy
I will do this by analyzing data and giving presentations on possible future business trends in business,
so that organizations can continually change to meet the needs of their customers.

CHAPTER 6

The Science of Mental Rehearsal

"Imagination is the preview of life's coming attractions."
– Albert Einstein

DAVE'S STORY

It was 2004, and things were just starting to take off in terms of speaking and coaching. Mental rehearsal had made a HUGE difference. I thought, *I wonder what else I could apply this to? Who would I most like to meet in the world? I'd love to meet Richard Branson, the Founder of Virgin.* I started doing what I did every evening, which was to visualize. I wrote in my journal. I practiced my gratitude exercises.

I just tagged this little vision onto the end where I imagined myself sitting down with Richard Branson and saw us shooting the breeze like two long lost friends. I did that for about two weeks and then I had this feeling, "You know what? That's it. It's out there. If it happens, awesome. If it doesn't, that's ok too."

Six weeks later, my then girlfriend came running into my office. She said "Guess what? We've been invited to an exclusive Virgin party. I said,

"Okay let's go!" Apparently, Richard Branson was NOT going to be there. I checked inside and then said, *"Let's still go anyway."*

A couple of weeks later, on a typical overcast UK day, we attended this outdoor Virgin event. As it turned out, Richard Branson WAS there. There were also hundreds of other people there. The organizers had made it very clear to us, in no uncertain terms, that nobody would be talking directly to Branson. My girlfriend looked at me. "You heard that, right?"

I nodded, but I was thinking, "There's too much synchronicity here." The day went on and sure enough nobody was getting near this guy. He was being whisked from one meeting to another. He had his entourage around him and was protected by bodyguards. I thought to myself, *It looks like it's not meant to be this time around. Maybe another time.*

Then I heard this voice inside, saying, *Hey, kid, it ain't over till it's over.*

There was one hour left at this lavish affair. Suddenly, I turned my head and had to do a double take. Twenty feet away there was Branson, sitting down, eating with a plastic knife and fork on an outdoor table. No one was around him. My girlfriend shook her head at me, but I remembered that one of Richard Branson's biggest secrets to success was boldness. I'd just read an interview with him in Fortune magazine where he had said this. I told myself, *I think he'd be very disappointed if I didn't give this my best shot.* So, I started to make my way towards him. It was like a scene out of *Mission Impossible.* I was expecting bodyguards to come out of nowhere and pounce on me. I took my first 5 steps. He didn't see me. He was eating and not coming up for air. I took another 5 steps. No bodyguards. Another 5 steps. I was just 5 feet away. I could literally hear the sound of the grass crunching beneath my feet. He still hadn't seen me so I cleared my throat. Nothing. I cleared my throat again, this time louder.

He looked up at me with an intense stare, kinda like the Terminator. He slammed his plastic knife and fork on the table. I had a moment of self-doubt and panic there and then, wondering whether should I take off or seize the moment. This could be an absolute disaster, or it could be life changing.

I said, "Mr. Branson. Big fan. Just wondering if we could have a chat for a few minutes."

Long pause. I could hear my heart pounding in my chest. It seemed like an eternity. He was looking at me, sizing me up. Suddenly, he smiled and said, "Sure. Have a seat."

We sat and chatted for 45 minutes. It was exactly how I'd seen it in my visualization where we were chatting like two long lost friends. What amazed me was that he completely focused his attention on me and it wasn't about him at all. It was such a surreal experience. I told him I was a speaker and performance coach, so he asked me to teach him something that I would teach my audiences. I showed him an exercise that demonstrates the power of the mind, and he loved it.

Towards the end of our conversation, he asked, "*So can we keep in touch? What's your email address? I want to send you some of my best secrets.*"

I enthusiastically gave him my email address. This was one of those magical moments in time. And it reaffirmed everything that I was doing in my life. We shook hands and took some pictures. Then, like a scene out of a James Bond movie, his entourage whisked him off to his helicopter and he flew away. True to his word, 2 weeks later he emailed me his top secrets of success.

WHAT IS MENTAL REHEARSAL?

Mental rehearsal is a way of pre-experiencing success, to visualize your end result and experience it ahead of time. Mental rehearsal is to imagine what it would be like to have achieved your goal and to start thinking, feeling, believing and acting as if it had already happened. It ties in beautifully with our lesson on believing without doubt, as if you've already achieved your result. This is the actual practice of doing it.

Many people associate mental rehearsal with professional athletes. Sports psychologists discovered years ago that if an athlete mentally rehearsed performing at his or her best, it was far more likely to play out like that. Practicing the sport physically AND rehearsing the sport mentally gave the athlete a huge winning edge.

You can do that with all kinds of things, not just sports. Anything where the pressure is high to succeed, where the survival brain easily gets triggered. You'll see top performers in public speaking, music, acting, negotiations, politics, and leadership, all doing this. Even people in their personal lives do it, for example, when preparing for an interview, going on a first date or meeting a writing deadline.

Modern science shows us that whenever we do something new or different we create brand new neural pathways to enable us to access the experience easily. Then, every time we repeat a behavior we strengthen the associated neural pathway. This is why it is so important to mentally rehearse success.

World champion athletes have won thousands of races in their own minds before ever setting foot on a track. It is the same with pro golfers and top ranked tennis players. Anyone who wants to achieve great things must first learn how to mentally rehearse.

BECOME AN EXPERT AT MENTAL REHEARSAL

One of the best habits I ever learned in my life was to become an expert at mental rehearsal. At first, I thought it was something I could do for five minutes on a Friday afternoon, and all would be good. But I noticed that did not change my life in any significant way. To live the life I truly wanted, I needed to become a master of mental rehearsal. I needed to place it high on my values list and practice regularly.

It's where I imagine myself in my ideal life, where I'm thinking the thoughts of that life, and therefore feeling the feelings of that wonderful life. This isn't about being delusional, living in a fantasy realm and ignoring the here and now. It's about being able to navigate both worlds. You're here and you're there. This creates a kind of "energetic bridge" between the present reality and the possible reality.

I am able to imagine that I'm already in that place. There is no doubt; it's only a matter of time. I'm living into my vision every day. I get this easy feeling, so I don't have to get uptight or worried that it won't happen. I KNOW with absolute certainty it will happen. That's the magical place to get to.

Why is that so important? Because when I take action from that place, I already have access to the thoughts and feelings that are going to create it. It becomes a joyful adventure to overcome the obstacles and move towards my vision, rather than a difficult task full of stress.

WHAT IF I CAN'T VISUALIZE?

Some people say to me, *I can't visualize*. Everyone has the ability to see pictures. To prove this to yourself, answer the following question: *What does your front door look like? What color is it? Which side is the handle on?*

In order to answer this question, you had to go into your imagination and create a picture. For most people, the picture will not be of 'photo' quality. And for the vast majority of people, the vision of what we want for our lives is usually hazy and out of focus. But with practice, you can learn to improve the quality.

Often, it is the things we DON'T want that are easy to visualize. They tend to be bigger, clearer, brighter and filled with emotions such as fear and doubt. It's a strange irony that our greatest fears often become our realities because these are our dominant thoughts. We allow them too much headspace and therefore bring them into reality. Our dreams and desires are often forced back into a small corner of our minds and are stored away with little emotional attachment.

SUPER ACHIEVERS PRACTICE MENTAL REHEARSAL

All truly great people throughout history have practiced mental rehearsal. They have purposefully used their imagination to access the creative realm – an underused integral part of us all. The great inventor, Thomas Edison, could design a machine perfectly in his mind and operate it mentally for years before ever creating it in real life.

Einstein imagined riding through space on a beam of light. Walt Disney entered the creative realm daily for ideas and inspiration; he could see pictures very vividly. Right from when she was a young girl, Oprah Winfrey decided that she would be a millionaire by the time she was 32. It became a self-fulfilling prophecy.

IMAGINATION RULES THE WORLD

By tapping into the subconscious mind, you are engaging your imagination. This can be hard for some people because many adults have been taught to believe that imagination is just for children. You play make-believe when you're young and that's okay. Once you're an adult you should put imagination away in a box, and just focus on being 'realistic'. Yet, all great inventions, businesses, speeches, music, art, relationships and movements started in someone's imagination. Take it out of the box and let it live again. Imagination rules the world!

HOW OFTEN SHOULD I MENTALLY REHEARSE?

The subconscious mind never sleeps, ever, so visualize every single chance you get. Make a habit of mentally rehearsing 5-10 minutes twice a day.

Waiting in a line? Do your favorite mental rehearsal.
Going down an elevator? Do your favorite mental rehearsal.
First thing when you wake up in the morning? Do your favorite mental rehearsal.

Lying in bed before falling asleep? Do your favorite mental rehearsal.

These small moments spent directing your mind can be life-changing. It is extremely powerful to access the subconscious mind, especially first thing in the morning and last thing at night. At MindStory Academy, our favorite tool for mental rehearsal is called a Neuro-Blueprint.

Neuro-Blueprints have been our secret weapon for the last 20 years. They do away with conventional visualizing altogether. The combination of deep relaxation, active meditation, mental rehearsal, hypnotherapy, neuro-repatterning phrases and just allowing our voices to guide you, along with beautifully composed musical scores have been proven over and over again with thousands of our clients worldwide to accelerate their success much faster than they can by themselves - taking their business and life to a whole new level. They are like mental rehearsal and visualization on steroids.

NERVE CELLS THAT FIRE TOGETHER, WIRE TOGETHER

We know that when we think the same thoughts or perform the same actions over and over, we repeatedly stimulate specific networks of neurons in particular areas of the brain. As a result, we build stronger, more enriched connections between these groups of nerve cells. This concept in neuroscience is called Hebbian learning. The idea is simple: Nerve cells that fire together, wire together. We can make our thoughts so real that the brain changes to look like the event has already become a physical reality. We can change it to be ahead of any actual experience in the external world.

Further research has shown that imagery can produce better performance outcomes and have a positive effect on anxiety, motivation, and self-efficacy. With mental rehearsal, the brain does not know the difference between physically doing the activity and imagining the activity. The idea that we can change our brain, and therefore the results in our life, just by thinking, has enormous implications.

BECOME FRIENDS WITH THE "QUANTUM FIELD"

Modern scientists are now acknowledging these findings. It is not woo-woo, New Age or wishful thinking. As we mentioned earlier, more and more the Quantum Field is a scientific fact. There is a field of energy that connects all living things. It is also a fact that our inner feelings, thoughts and beliefs all have an effect on the Quantum Field.

Napoleon Hill referred to it as the infinite intelligence, and it has been taught and referred to throughout time by some of the greatest business and spiritual giants, such as Andrew Carnegie, Henry Ford, Thomas Edison, Norman Vincent Peale, Gandhi, Mother Theresa, Nelson Mandela and many more.

When we mentally rehearse, the nervous system thinks it is actually having the experience and so the signal that goes out to the Quantum Field is that the imagined experience has already happened. Each imagining is a possible new timeline. If imagined clearly enough, in the right way, the timelines collapses, and the imagined reality becomes the actual one.

It doesn't matter what religious, spiritual, or philosophical background or viewpoint you come from. It doesn't matter how you describe it: imagination practice, visualization, mental imaging, or, using my favorite terminology, entering the Theatre of your Mind. What's important is that you do it!

HOMEPLAY

Follow the steps below and create a clear mental picture of the future you want for yourself. If you move towards it in a state of belief and expectation, never looking down, never doubting, no matter what your current circumstances, it will happen for you.

Many people find they get better results if they imagine themselves sitting before a massive cinema screen and imagining that they are seeing a picture of their goals as having already come about.

Think of yourself as being the director, the producer and the star of your own box office movie.

The important thing is to make these pictures as vivid and as detailed as possible. You want your mental pictures to approximate actual experience as much as possible.

As we mentioned earlier, research has discovered that the subconscious mind doesn't know the difference between what is real and what is imagined.

Stop and think about that for a moment; it is truly staggering. We are what we believe we are. Surely then it makes sense to build a mental vision that represents the very best version of yourself. Create that movie image in full, glorious surround sound technicolor and involve all of your senses. See it, feel it, hear it – and pay attention to the smallest details in your imagined environment.

The more excitement, passion, desire and intensity that you can create, the greater your emotional connection, the more quickly and completely it will become your reality.

Every detail of the imagined environment is important. You are creating a practice experience, and if it is vivid enough then your inner self, your subconscious mind, will believe it is an actual experience.

STEP ONE

Take a pad and pen and write out a brief outline or description of the mental movie you intend to construct, experiment with, develop, and view in the Theatre of YOUR Mind.

Set the dates that you intend to reach your goals. Make the goals personal and present tense as though you have already achieved them.

Use words that create emotion such as happy, excited, grateful, elated, passionate, fulfilled, content and thrilled.

Example: it is now _____ (date and time).

I am so excited that I have now made (insert your own figure).

I am so happy and grateful to be

_____

_____

_____

_____

_____

STEP TWO

Set aside 5–10 minutes a day, preferably at the same time each day to find a quiet, private place. Relax, close your eyes, enter your theatre, and begin watching, editing and replaying your movie.

With the end result playing as a movie you need to put yourself into the picture. Step out from the audience and become the star of the film. Be part of the movie, looking out at the future you have created. This is the end outcome that you are working towards.

Where are you?

What do you see?

What are you doing?

You need to be able to measure your success, to know that step by steady step you are moving forward towards your ultimate goals. Imagine achieving smaller goals along the way. Play it out in your mind in as much detail as possible. Create a rich, internal experience as though you are already living your future dream.

Make this vision real, vivid and detailed.

Feel it, live it, enjoy it!

Passion and emotion are the keys to motivation.

This is the difference between looking at your life as a magazine article or on a vision board and actually imprinting it where it boldly stands out in your mind and overshadows the negativity and doubt. If you can see it and feel it, then you are on a high-speed path to achieving it.

STEP THREE

Gradually perfect your movie so that you, as the star, perform exactly as you desire and achieve the experience and results you want.

For at least twenty-one days, keep playing this movie over and over. Practice mentally rehearsing until you are an expert at it.

Section 3

ACTION

ACTION

ACTION is Part 3 of the AVARA Coaching Model. Its about the action or inaction you tend to take as a result of a limiting MindStory. On the Empowering side, it's about brainstorming on a list of at least 7 things you could do, from this better MindStory. Usually, we stay stuck because our minds are used to only thinking of solutions from the past.

If you want a new result, you need to become a new person. The AVARA process helps your brain see the world in new ways. Once you've shifted your mindset, often you can see solutions you didn't see before. On the Empowering side of Action, any ideas goes. No editing. Let yourself write down obvious, bad, silly, strange ideas. Usually once you get those out of the way, often the truly innovative "out of the box" ideas start to surface. Have fun with it.

By doing this, you learn how to be comfortable moving out of your comfort zone, and receive the rewards of resilience where you bounce back from setbacks far more easily. Being a vision-oriented action-taker sets you apart as a powerful leader who influences with integrity, helping others to thrive.

You can start at ACTION in the model, especially if you have some form of PROCRASTINATION going on. For example, stalling, postponement, delaying of important goals. You might hear yourself say something like:

**"I can't seem to get myself started on a project
that's really important to me."**
"I'll focus on reinventing my business when I've made more money."
"I don't want to take action yet, in case it's the wrong direction."

Try using the model on your own area of procrastination.

Step A – Issue: What's a problem in your life? Describe the situation. No editing. We'll refer to this as your Limiting MindStory.

E.g. I said I wanted to write my book this summer, and it's already half over and I haven't even started. I seem to find everything else to do except writing. Each time I sit down to get started, I feel totally blocked.

Step B - Facts: Now see if you can state what you wrote above as objectively as possible. That means to separate facts from your interpretation, no adjectives, adverbs or descriptive phrases. Just the issue without your feelings or thoughts about it. From an outside perspective what would everyone agree on?

E.g. Book writing project I scheduled for this summer.

Step C – Limiting Version	Step D – Empowering Version
Now, you're going to break your MindStory down into its components parts here in the "Limiting Story" section. Then, we'll transform it in the "Empowering Story" section in the right-hand column. Start by going down this left column first, then go onto Step D, in the right-hand column.	Now that you've broken your MindStory down into its components parts, we'll transform it in this "Empowering Story". Look at what you wrote in each of the parts in the left column, and create a positive version here.
1) Acceptance: What are the limiting feelings, thoughts and meanings you are giving this situation. Express it like this *I am feeling* (negative feeling) *because* (negative thought). *I'm making this situation mean…* (your interpretation).	**1) Acceptance:** What are more empowering feelings, thoughts and meanings you could give to the situation? Express it like this *I have chosen to be* (positive feeling) *because* (positive thought). *A new meaning I could give this situation is…*
*E.g. **I'm feeling** stuck **because** I'm not sticking to my agreement with myself about writing the book this summer. **I'm making this mean** that I'm lazy and incapable of sticking to agreements with myself.*	*E.g. **I have chosen to** feel confident that I can stick to my agreements about writing the book. **A better meaning is** that I just need some structure, to break the project down into small sections, and to have an editor to work with.*

I AM FEELING	I HAVE CHOSEN TO BE
BECAUSE	BECAUSE
I'M MAKING THIS MEAN (List all, even if they seem unlikely or silly)	A BETTER MEANING (that would feel empowering to you)

2) Vision: What is your possible future A YEAR FROM NOW if you live from this limiting MindStory? Be specific.

E.g. I still have no book. It looks like I'll never get to fulfill this dream. I feel like such a failure.

2) Vision: What is your possible future A YEAR FROM NOW if you live from this more empowering MindStory? Be specific.

E.g. I've completed my book. it's out in the world and selling well. I'm getting great reviews. It's building my business in wonderful ways. I feel so proud of myself. It's making a big difference for people.

3) Action: What action or inaction is taking place? *E.g. I'm procrastinating on getting started.*	**3) Action:** What actions could you take to achieve this empowering VISION? Anything goes. No editing. List at least 7 ideas. Then choose 1 idea and break it down to specific, small next steps in Step E below. *E.g. Hire an editor* 1. 2. 3. 4. 5. 6. 7.
4) Reprogram: What is a recent event or experience that triggered this issue? Use present tense as if you were there now. *E.g. I'm sitting at my desk and someone sends me a funny YouTube video to watch. Two hours later I'm still looking at cute baby elephant videos.*	**4) Reprogram:** What is a similar event or experience that might happen in the near future where it's playing out in a more empowering way? Use present tense as if you were there now. *E.g. As soon as I sit down at my desk I turn off all programs and notifications, and I start writing immediately. I feel so inspired and on purpose.*

5) Attention: What are the limiting beliefs here or negative Self Talk? List all, even if they seem mean-spirited, unlikely or silly. *E.g. I don't have any discipline. Maybe I'm afraid of hard work, or success or failure. I'm just one of those people too afraid to put myself out there.*	**5) Attention**: What might be your new beliefs or Self Talk from this more empowering MindStory? Start your sentence with "Every day in every way I'm…" *E.g. Every day in every way I'm developing the habit of prioritizing my writing and I just follow through and do it.*

Step E - Specific Next Actions: Pick one idea from your empowering ACTION section above. What are 1 to 3 specific, small, next steps to get that started? Give each a date, delegate where possible. By breaking down big goals into small steps, it makes them feel easier to accomplish.

#	Action	Who	When
Eg	*Call my sister-in-law's editor to get a quote*	Me	Today
1.			
2.			
3.			

CHAPTER 7

Breaking Free of Negative MindStories

If you do not run your subconscious mind yourself,
someone else will run it for you.
- Florence Scovel Shinn

CARLA'S STORY

Remember when my public speaking teacher told me I was too serious? I agreed with her and decided that I had to change. I signed up for a comedy improvisation class. Have you ever done something like that? Think of shows like, *Whose Line is it Anyway*?

It was hard at first, but after awhile I started to develop some solid skills. That's when I got hooked. I loved spending a whole afternoon laughing. I would feel so much happier the rest of the day. I began taking two classes a week, then three, and then four. Finally, I quit attending the university, much to my parent's chagrin, just to focus on comedy.

I eventually went on to have my own comedy troupe. We performed sketch comedy and improvisation at various venues. One day, we were finishing up a show, taking our bows, and a woman gave us a standing ovation. It turned out to be my public speaking teacher. She came backstage to say hi. She said, *"I see you took my advice. That was very funny. You can come back to my class now."*

She also mentioned that I didn't even look the same. I looked younger, happier and healthier. I explained how my whole life had indeed changed. I'd lost the extra weight; I'd given up caffeine, alcohol and cigarettes. My skin allergies were gone. I was feeling fulfilled, more easygoing, more compassionate towards myself and others. I even wore brighter colored clothes. I now also had a great community of friends. There's an old saying, "Lighten up and your life will flourish because people get attracted by the light."

Was that all from quitting the university class and doing comedy? No, but that MindStory shift helped me do an external shift. I changed the core character, scripts and MindStories that I had been living by.

WE LIVE IN STORIES LIKE A FISH LIVES IN WATER

I went on to study playwriting, screenwriting and creative writing. This meant learning story structure and how stories affect the listener. I discovered that we live in stories like a fish lives in water. For example, on average, people spend 60% of their waking lives telling stories. Maybe you can relate. You're talking to your spouse about something that happened that day. You're sitting around the dinner table talking about your crazy aunt. You're also telling stories to yourself throughout the day and giving meaning to the experiences you have.

Ask yourself this question: Are you telling stories that are empowering and supportive, or are they disempowering and unsupportive? Most people are telling disempowering stories, and it's happening subconsciously, below their awareness. Making conscious choices around this habit can entirely change your life for the better.

I'll use a theater metaphor, because a lot of people can relate to that. You've probably acted in a play or a show at some point in your life. You put on a costume. You had a little script to recite. In my twenties, not only did I do comedy improvisation, I also acted in plays. Once I put on my costume and rehearsed my lines, I started to morph into that character. It was good preparation for doing a great performance.

If you have ever acted in a play, maybe you'll relate to this phenomenon, too. If the play went on for awhile, like over a month, I noticed that the character started to spill over into my regular life. Once I played a character who was stuck in hell during the entire play. It was by Jean-Paul Sartre and it was called *No Exit*. I noticed that I had a hellish experience in my regular life during that time, feeling stuck and frustrated and in conflict with many people around me. Then, when the play ended, that feeling disappeared.

We constantly take on characters and follow scripts in our lives. As Shakespeare proclaimed, "All the world is a stage, and all the men and women are merely players."

The next play I was in, I had the role of a fairy godmother in a pantomime. My job was to go around and make everybody's lives happier with my magic wand. This also spilled over into the rest of my life. I started looking for how I could make other people's lives better. That change in role, ironically, led me to the career I have today, which was far better than anything I could have imagined for myself at the time. I'll tell you how that happened a bit later.

ARCHETYPAL CHARACTERS AND SCRIPTS

As we said, the brain organizes itself in story form. There are many components of a MindStory, such as archetypal characters, core beliefs and scripts. An archetype is a term coined by the famous psychoanalyst, Carl Jung. Consider it similar to a software program or an app that you load onto your device. It's full of instruction sets for implementing specific objectives. We forget that we can load and delete these apps as we choose. In fact, we have choice around all of these components. We aren't stuck with any of them. The problem comes if you ignore this ability to upgrade your MindStories, or you only remove part of them, such as one or two components. That's like removing only one line of code in a Malware app. It's still going to make your computer underperform.

ARE WE LIVING IN A SIMULATED REALITY?

Some people believe that life is a simulated reality. There have even been some scientific papers proving it. Let's say that life is just a game where we're here learning certain life skills in some kind of virtual reality playground. We were also given amnesia when we arrived in the game to give us a kind of "game handicap," so we would stay focused and learn.

If that's true, then perhaps we go into the proverbial costume room of this simulated reality and choose a character to play around with. There are literally thousands of characters you could choose. Some people choose the Beggar, others choose the Orphan, or the Victim, or the Lost Girl, or the Hero, or the Guide.

Unconsciously, when I was younger, I latched onto The Orphan, The Victim and The Lost Girl. My parents split up when I was young, and they were both very busy and didn't have a lot of time for kids. So, I basically raised myself. I remember at 12 years old, if I wanted clothes, I had to make the money doing a paper route and pay for them myself. If I had to go to the dentist, I had to take a 45-minute bus trip there by myself. Other kids didn't have to do that. Their parents drove them there!

When I was older, I saw that circumstance as a gift because I had become much more independent, at a much younger age than most. At the time, however, I thought it meant there was something wrong with me. I was shuffled between neighbor's homes. Past a certain age, I was left to my own devices. I had no curfew and I just felt like The Orphan, The Lost Girl and The Victim. Another person in the same circumstance might have chosen different archetypal characters to take on.

WHAT IS A MIND VIRUS?

The archetype of The Orphan comes loaded with scripts and tends to spawn other disempowering scripts. Scripts are like your core motivation. Directors are always asking their actors to focus on their character's *core motivation* in each scene; otherwise, the scene will lose its impact.

The Orphan's core script is usually, *I'm not good enough*; otherwise, my parents would be around. That spawned The Lost Girl. Her script was, *I'm confused about where to go and what to do*. Feeling like a Lost Orphan made me a good target for bullies. That spawned The Victim, whose script was, *Why do bad things keep happening to me?* One archetype tends to lead to the others and becomes what we call a *Mind Virus*. Living out these negative archetypes can go on for years for people, as it did for me. It's like saying to the Director of a play, "I'd like to be the Lost Orphan in your play for decades, please."

While studying playwriting and acting, I had a transformational idea. It occurred to me that I could change these inner story components. The archetypal character was like my self-image, and the scripts were like instruction sets in a software program. These make up the component parts of a MindStory.

Your most commonly used characters then become your inner committee members. They are like the members of the board on your inner organization. They make decisions on your behalf for good or for bad. Most of this is happening below the threshold of your conscious awareness. Sometimes you need to fire certain board members and hire better ones.

HOW DO YOU CHANGE A MINDSTORY?

How do you break free from the unsupportive MindStories? You may have heard of the Hero's Journey, which was a whole structure of storytelling that myth expert, Joseph Campbell, identified. He researched stories in all cultures, throughout history, and noticed that humans tell the same basic story. The compelling stories that get told over and over again and get passed down through the generations tend to have the same basic story structure. It's where the hero gets a Call to Action in some aspect of life. They get pulled out of their comfort zone. They have mentors and teachers that help them. They face enemies, challenges and temptations. They get stuck in the "Belly of the Whale" or what we might call "The Winter of Change". They engage in a final conflict. If they get through that, they return home a better, wiser, and more resilient person ready to help others. We go much deeper into the Hero's Journey in Chapter 10.

We are all going on Hero's Journeys throughout our lives. The problem is that sometimes we get stuck. We get stuck in the Belly of the Whale, or in the conflicts, or temptations, and we never make our way out of these stories to be the hero, to bring back the wisdom to the true self and others.

I remember telling the Director of the play, *No Exit*, that I wanted to leave the play. I wanted a new role. All the other actors agreed that they were tired of playing these characters stuck in hell. The director decided to mount a comedy pantomime and gave us all fun, uplifting characters to play. I thought about how I could maybe ask my Inner Director to give me a new role. Maybe the Inner Director is like my higher self, or some greater part of the world's wisdom. I tried saying to this Inner Director, "I'd like a better role," and that's what I got. The process of doing that is what this part of the book is all about.

Instead of playing The Orphan, I wanted the opposite. To me, that meant The Connector: the person who had friends, family, community and support. Instead of the Lost Girl, I wanted to be a Guide who had clarity of direction and helped others do the same. Instead of the Victim, I wanted to be the Hero of my own life, responsible for my own choices.

These archetypes and scripts became new, supportive MindStories, which acted like the antibodies healing me from the Mind Virus.

INSTALLING GOOD SCRIPTS

These new archetypal characters had, embedded with them, better core scripts. The Connector script is, *"I am good enough to be supported."* The Guide says, *"I know the way and I'm here to help others find it, too."* The Hero says, *"I rescue myself."*

Many people think, "I have to wait until something outside of me happens to change things." Almost always, however, the impetus comes from within. It's in the "Acceptance" part of the AVARA Model. You accept the truth of your feelings and interpretations, and then reconstruct them. It's very hard to change the external world, without changing those inner interpretations The external follows the internal and not the other way around. Most people don't realize it, or forget it. It's the exploration, deconstruction and re-construction of the MindStory. Only then does your external world start to change. That's easy to forget even for people who teach this topic.

YOU'VE ALREADY CHANGED YOUR MINDSTORIES MANY TIMES

You've already changed your MindStories many times throughout your life. How do you know that? Think of an external event in your life when your self-image seemed to go up or down dramatically. For example, I was asked to speak at a huge international conference when I was 30 and I got a standing ovation. After that, I began to think of myself as a good speaker. Before that, I thought of myself as just an average speaker. Was it the external event or an internal choice? I chose that new self-image. I'd received a standing ovation a year before but I had interpreted the situation differently. After the first one, I said to myself, "I got that standing ovation because of a good story I told. It's not about me and my abilities as a speaker."

It's always the meaning you give to those external events and the decisions you make as a result. Since you've done this many times before, you can do it again. We're just helping you do it consciously. Even if you think you do this consciously already, there are probably areas of your life where you can still apply these tools. The more tools, the better.

UNCOVERING LIMITING MINDSTORIES

The greatest minds and hearts on the planet simply have a different set of MindStories than the average person. Your results in any endeavor will always match your subconscious MindStories. If life is a game, you have control of the joystick. You can develop a MindStory that supports your vision or one that shackles you to failure.

With our help, we hope you can gain this kind of mastery over your mind.

To uncover disempowering Mindstories you need to be totally honest with yourself. You may think you are free of a limiting MindStory when you aren't. This is another way people get stuck. Sherry came to me for help to get ready for a high profile speaking engagement. She taught interpersonal communication and had studied personal growth topics for years. I could see that she was terrified, but she insisted she wasn't. I wanted to help her with the inner game work, but she insisted she had completely cured herself of all fears and neurosis.

It always seems impossible until it's done.

— Nelson Mandela

As she rehearsed her speech, the discomfort was obvious. I sensed that she didn't feel worthy of the money and status that went with this high profile speaking opportunity. Finally, a few days before the event she had an emotional breakdown, which led to an important breakthrough. It helped her see the old scripts and archetypes from her childhood that were still influencing her. Even after all her years of personal growth, the old fears came back to haunt her.

The good news was that by accepting that reality, we could then do a turn-around in the nick of time. The event ended up being a huge success. It was a good reminder that no matter how much inner work a person thinks they've done, myself included, the old MindStories may still surface.

Having a tool like the AVARA Model and the others we use at MindStory Academy, or ones you've successfully used in the past, are important to keep close at hand.

HOMEPLAY

An important step in forming your new, more empowering MindStory is to realize what your beliefs are and to question those that no longer serve a purpose. Otherwise, beliefs left unchallenged will continue to limit you.

Answer the following questions to the best of your ability.

1. **What is a goal or vision you'd like to achieve?** It could be a financial, life success, health, relationship or career goal.

   _____

   _____

2. **What disempowering stories are coming from the little voice inside?** Most of us talk ourselves out of our greatness before the day even begins. We tend to focus on the negative as in, 'another day of struggle in a life that I hate'. What happened when you first woke up this morning? Did you worry or doubt? If so, how did that sound? These are unique to every individual, but below are some of the ones that we frequently hear. Circle the ones that you identify with.

   > It's hard to make money.
   > I can't make money doing what I love.
   > I have to work really hard to be successful.
   > I'm not good enough; I don't have what it takes.
   > I'm not smart enough; other people are smarter than me.
   > I've got children, you don't understand.
   > I've got problems, you don't understand.

I'm too young.
I'm too old.
I don't have enough time.
I'm unworthy of success.
I just don't get the lucky breaks in life that others get.
I'm just not meant to make any money.
I guess I'm destined for a life of struggle.
It won't last, my luck will run out.
I'll never get out of debt.
I'm afraid of being rejected.
I'm fearful of what others will think.
I'm not very good at following through.
I'm not great at presenting.
I'm not a great leader.
I'm not an organized person.

_____

_____

_____

_____

3. **Looking back across your life, where do you think these limiting stories came from?**

_____

_____

4. **How have they limited your life in the past?**

_____

_____

5. **Assuming you were to hold onto these limiting stories for the next five years:**

    How would they limit your future?

    _____

    _____

    How would they affect the quality of your life and relationships?

    _____

    _____

    How would they impact your finances?

    _____

    _____

6. **How can you start the day with a new MindStory?** For example,

    I'm so happy and grateful for the support I'm going to get today
    Another day where I've moved closer towards my big vision
    What an amazing time to be alive and to contribute to making
    the world a better place

7. **Turnarounds:** If some of the negative scripts above rang true, you could simply do a turnaround on them. You may not believe them at first, but after awhile you could hypnotize yourself into believing them, through repetition. Remember, it's just a game. For example,

    It's easy to make money.
    I can easily make money doing what I love.
    I can be successful and live a balanced life.

I'm good enough; I have what it takes.

I'm smart enough.

I've got children, and they'll help inspire me to succeed.

I've got problems, and these are helping me learn and grow.

I'm young so I have lots of time to succeed at this.

I'm older, so I have lots of wisdom now.

I have enough time.

I'm worthy of success.

I get the lucky breaks in life.

I'm just meant to make good money.

I'm destined for a life of success.

I'll easily get out of debt.

I can easily rise above any obstacles or rejection along the way.

I'm very good at following through.

I'm great at presenting.

I'm a great leader.

I'm an organized person.

---

8. **Who do you know who has accomplished this goal or vision?**
Thinking of the success of others can help build your belief that it's possible. If there is someone you feel envious of, that's a good place to take a look. Instead of the negative emotion of envy, think of how they could be an inspiration for you to achieve something similar or better.

---

9. **What MindStories do they hold that are different than yours?**
   You may have to guess, but most of us are far more intuitive than
   we realize.

   _____

   _____

   _____

   _____

10. **What difficult things have you accomplished before?**
    Acknowledging your own successes helps you build belief in
    your ability to achieve important goals. Belief is the engine of
    manifestation.

    _____

    _____

    _____

    _____

Your answers to these questions are starting to build your more empowering
MindStory at the neural network level of your brain. Imagine those new
neural networks of empowering MindStories forming and building
strength.

CHAPTER 8

Using Fear As Fuel

"Begin doing what you want to do now. We are not living in eternity. We have only this moment, sparkling like a star in our hand—and melting like a snowflake."
– Francis Bacon

DAVE'S STORY

You'll recall that my big dream was to become world class at speaking, selling and coaching to help people free their minds and live more purposefully. But there was one real problem with this. I had a deep fear of public speaking. I'm an introvert by nature, like a lot of speakers actually.

And I know exactly where this fear came from. I was 7 years old, in my annual school Christmas pantomime, and we were doing a play about the 1916 Irish rebellion. All I had to do was walk out on stage, unscroll my parchment and say, "Larry O'Lee" and "Tuatal O'Clay," and walk off. So, imagine the scenario. I was excited. I was ready. I had practiced. My parents were in the front row, my friends, teachers, other parents were all there watching… so the pressure was on.

I ran out to deliver my lines and suddenly I saw my parents and everyone else, and my mind went completely blank. Everyone burst into laughter and I went running off stage, completely humiliated. I made a decision at that time that I couldn't do any kind of public speaking without embarrassing myself. I would rather die than speak in public. That became a program that was still running in the background well into my twenties.

I kept stumbling along doing public speaking anyway, because I had this vision of doing it confidently one day. I knew that public speaking would help me sell more in my job, but it was also in alignment with my big vision. I had a vision of myself speaking to thousands of people, inspiring them to break through their limitations and step into their greatness.

This chapter is about how I overcame my fear of public speaking. As a matter of fact, it's a great process for getting over any fear.

BREAKING OUT OF THE SAFETY ZONE

We all seem to experience fears such as fear of failure, fear of success, fear of embarrassment, humiliation, or worrying about what other people think. It's endless. Fear is often what holds you back from succeeding in life. If you want to be successful, then it's essential for you to transcend those fears.

Even as entrepreneurs, most of us stay within the safety of our comfort zone. You might have stepped beyond your initial boundaries in order to follow your dream, but then you most likely constructed a new safety zone around yourself.

Mostly, we all think the same thoughts and perform daily in the same ways. It all feels very comfortable again. What starts to happen is, you get excited and set big goals. Awesome! You say to yourself, *I want to take my life to a whole new level. I want extraordinary success and to fulfill my true potential.*

You set your outcomes and write down your goals.

This is how much money I want to make.
This is what I want my business to look like.
This is what I want my life to look like.

Again, awesome. You are doing all the right things. But, at the same time, as you initiate all the positive actions, you are likely to unleash an internal civil war.

INTERNAL CIVIL WARS

The pre-frontal cortex, the creative part of your brain thinks, "I'm so happy and grateful to succeed beyond my wildest expectations."

Then, however, the reptilian, survival brain is programmed to stop anything that is unfamiliar or that might be uncomfortable. To move toward new goals and dreams, you must leave the familiarity of the known.

This doesn't just happen at the beginning of goal setting; it happens throughout a goal manifestation process. For example, let's say you're getting closer to goal completion, such as launching a new product. You are within sight of the finishing line; everything is going well and you can see your vision is gradually becoming a reality. Suddenly, the survival brain activates and the self-sabotage triggers go off.

HIGH ACHIEVERS ALSO HAVE FEARS

I want you to recognize that high achieving people also have fears, but they use those fears as fuel to propel them forward along their path. Usually, before every major breakthrough in life or in their business, they expect the inner pushback. It's part of the alchemical process of transformation. It's part of the hero's journey.

If you have ever been on stage or done public speaking, you know that nervous feeling, sometimes called butterflies in the stomach. That's the vagus nerve being activated by the survival brain. The vagus nerve is the longest cranial nerve. It runs all the way from the brain stem down to the stomach. This energy can help you, as long as you don't try to suppress it, or judge yourself for having it. In many case, once you step onto the stage the feeling fades and you begin to enjoy the experience.

You show me somebody who has zero fear in a high stakes situation, and usually they fail to learn and grow. You have to have some pressure within your life. You have to have something at stake to drive you to better yourself. It's that willingness to get uncomfortable at times that is part of the Hero's Journey. In other words, that kind of fear in its raw form is natural. It's the resistance to the fear that makes it become unhealthy.

If you want to be more than average and create a life that matches your vision, then it helps to do things every day that might make you a little uncomfortable.

FEEL THE FEAR AND DO IT ANYWAY

As the saying goes – *Feel the Fear and Do It Anyway.*

As we discussed earlier, you can Mentally Rehearse a high stakes activity and visualize the outcome that you want. Your imagination has the power to absolutely change your nervous system's reaction to a high pressure situation.

IDENTIFYING "FEAR IMPRINTS" FROM THE PAST

If you have a huge, overwhelming fear response its usually because something has happened in your past. It was likely an experience that you interpreted in a negative way, and that you never fully learned from. If so, then the experience becomes lodged in the subconscious and stored as trauma. The survival brain then goes on autopilot to avoid similar situations. Just remember that sometimes the disappointment, upset or humiliation that you experienced in childhood was a choice. It was an interpretation. Someone else in the same situation might, at some point, choose to interpret it differently.

Carla's mother was a social worker who worked with troubled teens. It was fascinating to her that two children could come from the same dysfunctional home, and one would go on to live a purposeful and healthy life, and the other would live a destructive and unhealthy life. Same situation, different interpretation, which led to a different result in life.

Even small setbacks as a child can make people very reactive as an adult. One of our coaching certification students, Andrew, said he didn't have many friends at school. In retrospect he saw that was probably because he was shy. People assumed his lack of friendliness meant he didn't like them, so they excluded him from social activities. He felt rejected many times as a child.

Fast forward to the present day, and he was getting triggered in any situation that might involve rejection. At the survival brain level, it felt like potential death. Even though he knew logically that he would NOT actually die if he made calls to prospects, it still felt like that at a bodily, somatic level. It is a sad truth that unless we reinterpret these past events, we stay stuck getting triggered over and over again.

When we are young, in the period of time we call *the imprint period*, which is generally up to the age of seven, negative things sometimes happen to us. We learn fear responses to various things like speaking in public, being told off, getting in trouble, being excluded, getting bullied, failing an exam or being rejected.

Some of you reading this book will have very little memory of your childhood, the good or the bad experiences. Even if you forgot that it happened, it can still have a detrimental effect on your psychological and physiological well-being. The trauma can stay lodged in your nervous system and cells.

It also might be that you clearly remember instances of fear, pain, embarrassment or humiliation. I had another client, Elizabeth, who was forced to stand on a chair and read out loud to the class as a punishment for talking in class. Her brain made a connection between being in front of people and that horrible feeling of fear and humiliation. There is nothing you can do to prevent it from happening; it is a built-in self-preservation mechanism. You may be familiar with irrational fears or phobias. The mind just photographs it once and it becomes imprinted, so one negative experience can lead to a lifelong terror of spiders, dogs, heights, water or whatever. The fear is irrational, but it can also become overwhelming. It is an unconscious response that has become part of your internal programing.

Whatever you fear today that seems excessive, like selling or dealing with authority figures or talking to a group of people, you are being held back by something from your earlier years. You are responding in the present with negativity inherited from your past.

You need to address this now. It is time to change the programming.

HOMEPLAY

The key to overcoming fear is taking massive action. However, this can be too much of a jump for many people who have been avoiding taking important actions. Here are 6 key steps you can take to move you towards taking massive action.

1. HONOR THE FEAR

Unconditionally accept where you are right here, right now, in the moment. This is the door opener.

As long as you're worried about your future, which is what fear and anxiety are, you are going to be without your power. All your energy is going into the fears. Your brain can never work effectively in this climate.

So, if you're fearful of taking action in certain areas right now, accept that this is where you are and be okay with it.

As soon as you accept this and allow yourself to feel the vibrational frequency of fear, it helps ground you into your body, where you can begin to transform it and access higher capacities.

What does the fear or anxiety feel like physically? Some people describe it as:

- A pain/tightness in the chest
- Nausea
- Upset stomach
- Trembling or shaking hands
- Restlessness and the inability to sit still
- Altered breathing, usually fast and shallow
- Sweating uncontrollably
- Dry mouth
- An uncomfortable warmth, feeling flushed
- Rapid heartbeat, often pounding in the ears
- Confusion and not being able to think straight
- A pins and needles sensation in the arms and legs
- Headache and general tension
- Teeth grinding/jaw clenching
- Feel like crying
- Restless sleep
- Agitation in the solar plexus

How does fear show up for you? Think of a situation that brings fear or anxiety and circle the ones on this list that are true for you. Add your own sensations at the bottom. If you feel fear right now just be present with the physical sensations of it.

_____

_____

_____

Most people resist these feelings in case they get engulfed by them. The irony is that by feeling them, they can finally get released from your cell structure and you can then use the energy as fuel for transformation. Then the feeling changes and no longer "owns" you.

As long as you are judging yourself and blocking the experience, you're actually using up vital life force energy to magnify the bad feelings.

2. LET GO OF THE FEAR

Accept your breathing as it is right here, right now, in the moment. The same way you accept the stars at night. Your breathing is a mirror of what's going on inside. Relax your breathing and relax yourself.

Concentrate on your breathing and focus on exhaling. When you focus on exhaling, just say the words…let go…let go…let go for 3-5 minutes. Do this, and you will be the most relaxed you have been for a long time.

3. REFRAME THE FEAR

Most of the fears we have are negative interpretations that are replaying on autopilot. Once you understand the cycle at play from a wiser perspective, it isn't as terrifying. One of our coaching certification students, Mary, had a fear of speaking up at a network event because of what others might think. Each person had to stand up and give their elevator speech for 60 seconds.

As she spent more time with that networking group, she came to realize that most people were so focused on how they were doing that they didn't even notice her speech. Each time she did the speech, she got better. Over time she reframed the experience in terms of it being a learning experience that most others had no strong opinion about, and that calmed her down. Now she is a master of the elevator speech and teaches it to others.

Part of the maturity and the mastery here is realizing that instead of focusing on the outcomes that are negative, we can start reframing our fears. We can start thinking, visualizing and placing our attention onto the things that would turn out to be wonderful and magnificent if we shift our focus and change our thinking.

4. FAST FORWARD WITH THE FEAR

Connect with your mission in life, connect with a fear much worse than the one occupying your mind now: like the fear of being on your death bed filled with regrets. For me, I can't think of a worse fear than that. I remind myself of my mission, that I'm here to show people how to unleash their personal greatness in this time when so many of us have forgotten what we're made of. I'm on fire for this mission…it's my purpose. Helping people achieve their highest vision is personal for me, to remind you that your days and mine really are numbered. Life is too short to play small with your potential.

5. USE THE FEAR AS FUEL

Think of the many times you were fearful and you still managed to take action and surprise yourself. Neuroscience shows us that you can actually use the epinephrine and the cortisol the fear releases to propel you forward and break the habit of procrastination. It's vital to understand that the natural process of any goal-setting sequence is to feel excited and fearful at the same time. In fact, these are similar feelings in the body – fear and excitement – if you really pay attention. One just has a more negative vibration and one has a more positive vibration. You can, therefore, switch from one to the other quite easily. It's simply a neurochemical switch that you can activate with your intention.

6. GIVE AND YOU SHALL RECEIVE

Look beyond yourself and serve. Stop worrying about whether you're good enough, ready enough, or perfect enough in order to start. Taking action can help others: your family, your business and your community. Serve! The way to get out of your head is to get in motion serving other people. Seek to add more value to the marketplace. Anytime you're lost in fear and want to switch to excitement you just need to change your thought. You go from "What if I fail?" to "What if I succeed and make a huge difference in people's lives?"

A NEW MODEL OF BUSINESS

The old model of business was based on scarcity: take as much from as many people as possible because there isn't enough for everyone to win. The new model is completely different. It's based on prosperity and abundance and the powerful ideal that the person who helps the most people wins. Give and you will receive. Once you really get this, everything in your life changes. Our lives come alive when we help others grow their dreams.

So remember these 6 tips:

1. **HONOR THE FEAR**
2. **LET GO OF THE FEAR**
3. **REFRAME THE FEAR**
4. **FAST FORWARD WITH THE FEAR**
5. **USE THE FEAR AS MOTIVATON**
6. **GIVE AND YOU SHALL RECEIVE**

CHAPTER 9

How to Fail Successfully

If you want to increase your success rate, double your failure rate.
– Thomas J. Watson

DAVE'S STORY

Remember in one of the earlier lessons how I got a phone call that changed my life forever? I had just emerged from my *dark six months of the soul*. I had made the decision that I was going to chase my dream of becoming a world class speaker and performance coach. Looking back, I realize that I had decided to fail forward and do what it takes, no matter what. I was practicing feeling the positive emotions I would feel ahead of time, as if I were already living my dream life. Then, suddenly, as often happens when you commit fully to something, I got a phone call out of nowhere. It was from my good friend, Kate.

She said, "Dave, I would like you to speak in front of my group." She had a personal development group, and she wanted me to talk about the power of the subconscious mind. She'd heard me do presentations on this before as part of my former job, and she loved what I had to say.

As I always had this vision of speaking and coaching people around the world on this topic, this then initiated a civil war inside - among my inner committee members. I call them my "brain characters." One member of my committee felt it was possible, that I could do this and was meant to do this. I like to call him "General Frontal Lobe." But, other members that sprung from my fear center kept squashing the idea. I call the main leader of this inner revolt "Colonel Amygdala."

Colonel Amygdala is responsible for keeping me safe and protecting me from dangerous situations. It's my fight or flight mechanism. Unfortunately, if left unchecked he can keep me too safe – not daring to venture outside of my comfort zone. So, whenever I want to go to a new higher level in my life, he panics and starts screaming, "Nooooo – you must not go for this higher vision. We're on course for mediocrity. Danger. Danger. Danger. You must STOP now. Nobody wants to listen to you. Who do you think you are? You have nothing to offer."

Isn't it ironic that when I was at one of my lowest points ever, I got this phone call? We've seen that so often with our clients. It's at times like this when you're so raw, when you are facing so much opposition, when there seems to be no light at the end of the tunnel, that it can seem like the easy way out is to quit. Colonel Amygdala yells "Danger!" Another of my inner committee members, Captain Motor Cortex, tried to distract me with low priority concerns (perhaps you would be better off re-organizing your paperclip drawer). The most miserable member of my inner saboteurs entouarge, Veteran Limbic, attempted to remind me of my past failures. Many times, in my past, all three of these 'characters' have managed to talk me out of my greatness.

This time, however, I decided to listen to General Frontal Lobe. Whenever I've listened to him before, he has always reminded me of what is possible. I had a feeling of lightness, when my heart opened ever so slightly. It was a familiar but long forgotten feeling.

This was not the same kind of heavy feeling I'd been used to for so long. I latched onto that feeling—I HAD to. When I looked at any breakthroughs I'd experienced in the past, I had a resistance to seizing the moment; but, when I ignored this resistance, I always seemed to break through to a higher level of success in my life - whether it was in my career, finances, relationships or lifestyle. It was almost like the universe was testing me, to see what I was made of, to test my commitment to my vision. In remembering that, I chose to say "yes" to Kate's offer.

For the weeks leading up to the presentation, I practiced mentally rehearsing the outcome 1 wanted. I saw myself delivering THE most impactful, inspiring and engaging talk of my life so far. I was seeing, feeling and hearing the end result with all the emotions of joy, excitement, gratitude, wonder, inspiration, satisfaction, relief, etc.

So, a few weeks later, there I was at this event with about 500 people in the room. The atmosphere was electric and, to my horror, on that night I was absolutely terrified. Colonel Amygdala and his best friends were having a field day reminiscing over my past failures – especially that time when I was laughed off the stage as a 7-year old kid. Have you ever thought you had overcome something once and for all, only to realize that it was still alive and kicking?

Unfortunately, none of the things I had used in the past to shake off the negativity were working. There I was in the restroom where I started doing my power moves and my positive anchoring techniques. Still, my heart was beating loudly in my chest, my mouth was dry, and I was sweating profusely. I went out, walked up to Kate, and said, *"I don't think I can do this."*

She said, *"Too late, Dave, you're up next!"*

I was behind the stage and the MC was announcing me: *"Ladies and gentlemen, we have a surprise guest this evening. Kate has invited this amazing speaker; you are going to love this guy. He's going to inspire you, he's going to motivate you, he's going to entertain you. Prepare to have your mind blown by the information you learn here tonight.*

Meanwhile, I was back stage dying… while all my committee members were having a great time. *How would I ever live up to that introduction?*

After the intro, I walked onto the stage to a thunderous round of applause. I looked out at the sea of faces. Everyone went silent, and you could hear a pin drop. I was still hearing Colonel Amygdala in my head, saying, *"This is going to be the worst disaster ever. You'll never get another speaking opportunity after this fiasco, etc."*

You won't believe what happened next. I'll tell you a bit later (it's not what you'd expect).

HOW TO FAIL SUCCESSFULLY

Most people give up too easily. They don't understand that the path to success is paved with failure. They don't realize how much it takes to succeed and the level of resilience necessary to achieve it. Learning to successfully fail is vital to building resilience and good mental health. In fact, sometimes you have to trick yourself and others to build this vitally important life skill.

The path to success requires discomfort, reflection, and overcoming past failures. This understanding of how to fail successfully has been a source of freedom for many of our clients. There's a lot of information about how to avoid failing and about how to succeed, but there's not enough information about how to fail properly.

To fail is deeply human. It's also deeply human to embrace, learn from, and transcend failure. Now, I consider a failure as something that didn't work the way I had planned, so I don't see it as such a negative thing anymore. It's merely an unmet expectation. I would say that most people don't achieve their dreams because of their inability to understand the role of failure.

Often, people say to me, "I have a real fear of failure," and I'll say, "Well, what does that mean? What are you afraid of?"

That's one of the things we do in MIC, our MindStory Inner Circle. We always try to get to the root cause of all the issues, rather than just fixing the surface symptoms.

Failure is just something that didn't turn out the way someone or many people had expected. But, what most people do is they just stop trying, and therefore they never fail. They keep their expectations really low.

"If you're not prepared to be wrong, you'll never come up with anything original."
- Ken Robinson

The biggest failures for me are the ones where I didn't even try to do something because I was so afraid of failing. There are a lot of things that I was really afraid to go after in the beginning. Many times I didn't say yes to a speaking opportunity because I felt I wasn't prepared; I was waiting for perfection. A lot of people are waiting for perfection.

Not trying is the biggest failure. I think Albert Einstein said it best. "You never fail until you stop trying."

WHY DO WE AVOID FAILING?

Why do we avoid failing? It always comes down to avoiding wanting to feel something negative. You want to avoid the pain of thinking certain thoughts that are going to create negative emotions. Often, the real reason why you avoid any kind of failure is because you don't want to feel judged or embarrassed or rejected or disappointed. At the core of it all, you don't want to feel those feelings about yourself.

There's a famous quote by Eleanor Roosevelt: "No one can make you feel inferior without your consent." If someone says, "I don't like your nose," you might get offended if you also don't like your nose. But if you like your nose, then it won't bother you. That's why it's almost NEVER about what other people say or think; it's usually ALWAYS about your thoughts and interpretations about yourself.

Perfectionism usually masks fear. It gives you an excuse to not take the action and risk failure.

The good news is that you can choose to change your interpretation, which would change your feelings. That's where the vast majority of people lack serious training. You get to decide what you're going to think about any person, situation, event, or experience. You get to decide what you're going to make an experience mean to you.

Now that doesn't mean you need to pretend that it's pleasant to fail or simply ignore the frustration that arises when a goal falls out of reach. But, accepting the feelings that come with failure, being curious about what caused them, and re-interpreting the situation in a more empowering way – are tools for a lifetime.

That said, when you set out to achieve a particular goal and you fall short and fail…what's the worst thing that could happen?

The worst thing that can happen is you may feel disappointed and then you can just go back to doing what you're doing now.

We can decide to make that actually mean something positive, and, therefore, you won't need to dread experiencing a negative emotion.

A better way of framing it would be to shrug your shoulders and say, "So what? All this means is that even bigger things are on the way."

The great inventor, Thomas Edison, is the perfect example of this. He was a prolific failure. Again and again, he tried and failed with his experiments. If he had been too focused on each one and allowed it to hold him back, we might never have had the electric light bulb. Edison held onto his vision and he saw every failed attempt simply as another stepping stone towards his success.

"I have not failed 10,000 times. I have not failed once. I have succeeded in proving that those 10,000 ways won't work. When I have eliminated all of the ways that it won't work, then I will find the way that it will work."
— Thomas Edison

When you think about it that way, it usually doesn't make you want to avoid failure. It makes you want to learn and grow and try it again. You're the one that's determining what failure means. It just means you didn't meet your own expectations. It's stepping back and taking a more objective, neutral position on the situation, which then allows you to make a new choice.

SUCCESS IS AN ALCHEMICAL PROCESS

Success, ironically, is one of those things that is acquired by being willing to fail. In other words, if you want to multiply your success by ten times, you need to multiply your rate of failure by at least that much – or more. You also need to multiply your willingness to learn from those situations by ten times, so that you get better at meeting your own expectations.

If you look back on your life, maybe you've noticed a pattern around achieving success. Think of an area of life where you did that; you triumphed in the face of challenges. Often, you can see a pattern of failures, learnings, trying again, more failures, feeling defeated, gathering courage again, more learnings; and, then, at a certain point in the game, in the alchemical process, it's just natural to achieve success.

The process of growth was complete and so success was inevitable. People don't realize that success is an alchemical process. It's the Hero's Journey in action. You just go through the steps. If you try to skip steps, it's like trying to bake a cake without the right ingredients, or without leaving it in the oven long enough. It comes out all wrong. Your sequence of efforts, failures, actions, learnings, courage and persistence become a game you discover how to play...and then success no longer feels like an outcome only given to a chosen few....but rather a game you know how to play.

HOMEPLAY

MAKE A NEW AGREEMENT WITH YOURSELF

Some don't want to take the necessary actions towards success because they know they'll beat themselves up if something goes wrong. One way to remedy that is to make an agreement with yourself. Write out an agreement like this and put it somewhere you can read it every day for 21 days:

MY AGREEMENT AROUND FAILURE

There's going to be a chance that along the way of achieving my goals, I'm going to fail, and probably many, many times. And that's ok. I'll still be supportive of myself and believe in myself. I'm going to treat myself with respect. I'm going to honor myself and my journey. I'm only human. I'm going to use those failures as an opportunity to learn and to be kind and compassionate with myself. I'm going to use them as an opportunity to love myself more instead of putting myself down.

Now, if you set yourself up for that ahead of time, before you start any kind of action, you're going to be much more willing to take the action and to take the risk that's required to succeed.

REVISIT YOUR MISSION

One of the best ways to fail successfully is to reconnect with your vision, values and mission. Your Mission is the path you take to get there and the specific means by which you accomplish your vision. It is comprised of who you are going to be and what you are going to do to reach your mountaintop.

My Mission is: _____

_____

E.g. *My Mission is to help people become a master of their mind so they can get their message out in the world and make a bigger difference while making a great living.*

REVISIT YOUR CORE VALUES

Core Values keep you true to your path and true to yourself. You steer your course based on what you believe in, your ethics, and what is most important in your life.

Knowing your values is essential, because happiness comes from living and acting in accordance with your highest values every single day. When you're happier, you're in flow. And when you're in flow, you do everything better.

Research on people at the end of their lives has shown that their greatest regret was not living their life to the fullest, not loving enough and not following their heart.

Think of someone you deeply respect. Describe 3 qualities in this person that you most admire. *E.g. They're loving, compassionate, wise, creative, courageous, forgiving, fun, warm, inventive, honest, authentic, loyal, adventurous, happy, carefree, persistent, etc.*

1.
2.
3.

Another way to discover your 3 core values is this. Fast forward to the end of your life. What will make you feel like you lived a good life? What are the values you lived by? What are people saying at your memorial service? What 3 qualities would you like to be best known for? See if you get the same ones or something different. *E.g. Committed, peaceful, graceful, open-minded, curious, free-spirited, community-oriented, self-sufficient, self-mastery, spiritual growth, etc.*

1.

2.

3.

REVISIT YOUR VISION

Close your eyes and see yourself living your mission and core values. Now, replay your vision in the theatre of your mind. Make sure you do it in glorious detail, as if you woke up in the future and everything you wanted had already happened. Feel your excitement, gratitude and sense of personal power at having achieved this.

Once a week repeat this exercise and you will find yourself becoming more resilient and able to embrace failure because there's a deeper meaning and greater sense of purpose to everything you do.

Section 4

REPROGRAM

REPROGRAM

REPROGRAM is Part 4 of the AVARA Coaching Model. It's about taking yourself back to a moment in time where the limiting MindStory is in effect. It's also about taking yourself into the future and doing a mental rehearsal of how you want your life to go instead in that same circumstance.

Here you learn to reprogram your subconscious mind. No amount of conscious will power will change your reality at the subconscious set point. For example, many people have subconscious set points around how much money they can make, or how much they weigh, or how successful they can be.

You may have experienced that phenomenon, where your willpower only gets you so far. You increase your income and then it snaps back to the old levels of income. You lose the weight and then you regain it all.

That's when you need to consciously identify the subconscious programs that control you, which the AVARA model can help you do.

You can start at REPROGRAM in the model, especially if you have some form of DOUBT going on. For example, mistrust, misgivings, skepticism, hesitation, self-doubt, doubt about others, doubt about a situation, etc. You might hear yourself say something like:

I have this goal for my life, but I just don't believe it's possible.
I'm not moving forward with my vision because
I don't trust that it will work out.

*I'll go after my dreams when I have (*insert reason
here – *e.g. more money, more time, etc.)*

Try using the model on your own area of DOUBT

Step A – Issue: What's a problem in your life? Describe the situation. No editing. We'll refer to this as your Limiting MindStory.

E.g. Just when I'm starting to get momentum with my new life coaching business, something sabotages it. I suddenly get anxious. It's like I'm expecting something bad to happen, and then I think I attract it.

Step B - Facts: Now see if you can state what you wrote above as objectively as possible. Separate facts from your interpretation. No adjectives, adverbs or descriptive phrases. From an outside perspective what would everyone agree on?

E.g. Building my life coaching business.

Step C – Limiting Version	Step D – Empowering Version
Break down this Limiting MindStory into its components parts here in the left hand column. Then, transform it in the "Empowering" column.	Look at what you wrote in the left-hand column, and create a more empowering version here.
1) Acceptance: What are the limiting feelings, thoughts and meaning you are giving to the situation? Express it like this *I am* (negative feeling) *because* (negative thought). *I'm making this situation mean...* (your interpretation). *E.g. **I'm feeling** confused about how to move forward with my business **because** of all the obstacles. **I'm making this mean** that something is trying to sabotage me, and I feel unsupported by Life.*	**1) Acceptance:** What are more empowering feelings, thoughts and meanings you could give this situation. Express it like this *I have chosen to be* (positive feeling) *because* (positive thought). *A better meaning I could give this situation is...* *E.g. **I have chosen to be** clear about how to move forward with my business despite the obstacles. **A better meaning** is that all businesses face constant obstacles. My job is to choose a direction as best I can, and course correct as I go.*

I AM FEELING	I HAVE CHOSEN TO BE
_____	_____
_____	_____
_____	_____
BECAUSE	BECAUSE
_____	_____
_____	_____
_____	_____
I'M MAKING THIS MEAN (List all, even if they seem unlikely or silly)	A BETTER MEANING (that would be more empowering to you)
_____	_____
_____	_____
2) Vision: What is your possible future A YEAR FROM NOW if you live from this limiting MindStory? Be specific. E.g. I've burnt myself out and given up on my dream. I've been forced to get a 9-5 job to make ends meet and I hate it.	**2) Vision:** What is your possible future A YEAR FROM NOW if you live from this more empowering MindStory? Be specific. E.g. I have a successful life coaching business. I earn more in one month than I previously earned in a year.

3) Action: What action or inaction is taking place? *E.g. I find I'm busy being busy doing a lot of things that have no real impact.*	**3) Action:** What actions could you take to achieve this empowering VISION? Anything goes. No editing. List at least 7 ideas. Then choose 1 idea and break it down to specific, small next steps in Step E below. *E.g. Better follow up with prospects.* 2. 3. 4. 5. 6. 7.
4) Reprogram: What is a recent event or experience that triggered this issue? Use present tense as if you were there now. *E.g. I'm close to landing a big coaching contract. Suddenly, I find myself worried and confused about how to really help the client. I end up sounding muddled on our strategy call, and so lose the chance to work with them.*	**4) Reprogram:** What is a similar event or experience that might happen in the near future where it's playing out in a more empowering way? Use present tense as if you were there now. *E.g. I'm close to landing a big coaching contract. I'm feeling confident, clear and in control of the conversation. I know how to really help them. I totally nailed it. They end up signing up with me.*

5) Attention: What are the limiting beliefs here or negative Self Talk? List all, even if they seem mean-spirited, unlikely or silly. *E.g. I just feel like I can't catch a break. I keep sabotaging myself. I don't want to try anymore. It's too difficult.*	**5) Attention**: What might be your new beliefs or Self Talk from this more empowering MindStory? Start your sentence with this progressive affirmation, "Every day in every way I'm..." *E.g. Every day in every way I'm attracting more of the right coaching clients who are a joy to work with.*

Step E - Specific Next Actions: Pick one idea from your empowering ACTION section above. What are 1 to 3 specific, small, next steps to get that started? Give each a date, delegate where possible. By breaking down big goals into small steps, it makes them feel easier to accomplish.

#	Action	Who	When
Eg	*Follow up with 3 recent strategy calls.*	Me	Friday
1.			
2.			
3.			

CHAPTER 10

Your Hero's Journey

'You are the *Hero of your own Story.*'
– Joseph Campbell

Many people who've lived a few decades look back on their life and see a series of failures. That's because the mind has a bias for negatively viewing the world. The problem is that a disempowering MindStory of your entire life will set you up for even more failure moving forward. Everyone has had ups and downs, periods where they felt stuck, and times when they felt triumphant. It's a varied journey. Try looking back at your life from the perspective of The Hero's Journey as Joseph Campbell outlined it. This can help you discover where exactly you're stuck and help you rewrite a more empowering MindStory of your entire life to help you move forward.

Just like there are neural pathways in the brain that fire in particular patterns, there is a system of energetic processes and 'instruction sets' that cannot be seen under a microscope, yet they're there. The mind organizes the rules by which we live in story form, with characters, scripts, motivations, plot, theme, setting, etc. A limiting MindStory has an ugly asymmetrical pattern to it like in the next image, whereas an empowering MindStory has a more beautiful and symmetrical pattern to it.

A LIMITING VERSUS EMPOWERING MINDSTORY

I believe we're supposed to have a beautiful MindStory to live by, but most people's original purpose, their roadmap, got corrupted along the way. It's important to get back to our true nature in order to truly live our purpose. Here we invite you to be like a technician, reconstructing the MindStory of your life back to its original symmetry and beauty. Use the Hero's Journey HomePlay at the end of this chapter to help you do that.

CARLA'S STORY

I found over the years of helping hundreds of clients find and tell their mission story, it could change their self-image in profound ways. Let me give you an example from my own life, in case it helps you do it for yourself.

Being a speaker and leadership coach was an unlikely career for someone like me. In my teens I was very shy, had been labeled dyslexic, and my family had recently broken apart. My mother left the family. She was tired of doing all the parenting, and she wanted her freedom. I'd taken her departure very personally, thinking she left because of me. My father was devastated, depressed and completely unprepared for trying to raise two rebellious teenage daughters, so he disappeared into this work. I took that personally, too, and developed low self-esteem as a result.

As a teen, I had no pocket money. The divorce created financial troubles for us. If I wanted to buy clothes, any necessities or movie tickets, I had to earn it myself. All through school I had many part time jobs from a paper route to a drug store clerk to a waitress. The best job I had was a banquet waitress at a university conference center. I loved it because I got to witness conference speakers. Most teenagers at the time never had the opportunity to do that. One event, in particular, changed the course of my life. The conference was about solving problems with the environment.

There I was, in my scratchy, polyester black and white uniform, at the back of the room, available to pour coffee for anyone who wanted it. The first speaker was a politician making promises about cleaning up the environment. He didn't seem very genuine and people were bored. The second speaker was an environmental activist shouting and blaming the government and corporations for polluting the environment. People were paying more attention, but they were frowning and crossing their arms.

The third speaker was a woman. I'd actually never seen a female speaker before. Dr. Helen Caldicott stood there looking frail and shy, but she seemed sweet natured. I could barely see her behind the lectern, but I could relate to her. My mother was the opposite in- big, bold and a warrior for social change. I felt she wanted me to be more like her, and I could never live up to her expectations.

Dr. Helen Caldicott seemed like another alternative for how to be in the world. Her book and documentary, *If You Love This Planet,* were fascinating. Nobody had heard of her before, so some conference goers started sneaking out the back of the room. She started with, "We can tax polluters and accuse politicians of lying, but that puts us at war with each other. My team and I have put together community action guides to clean up the environment at the grassroots level. It's very easy to get started."

Then, she told stories of how these guides were making a difference around the world. She showed images of people doing creative collaborative projects in communities to help the environment in Argentina, New Zealand, the UK, Zambia and Sri Lanka. The conference goers stopped, turned around, and started coming back into the room. She was suggesting we take collective responsibility for what was happening, to get into action together and to do it out of love, and not hate.

You could hear a pin drop as she spoke. People were transfixed. Mouths hung open, and tears rolled down the faces of some of the listeners. After she was done, there was a stampede onto the stage. People wanted to buy her film, get her book, fund her project, invite her to speak, and volunteer for her organization. You could sense they were moved by her humility, passion and the idea of working together as a community.

That day, I decided I could maybe become a speaker, too, who could positively influence people like that. I wanted to help galvanize people into community action, just like Dr. Helen Caldicott did that day. Literally, that one experience of seeing her speak altered a thousand decisions I've made since then.

At that time, there were hardly any women on the speaking circuit, so it was an unlikely choice for a teen girl. But, after that I became inspired, and I sought out opportunities to do this kind of work.

What happened to me, however, was kind of ironic. While I was in university, I got a few different summer jobs that involved public speaking. It became very clear that my dyslexia and shyness were getting in the way. Public speaking was clearly a job for an extrovert with high self-esteem, not an introvert full of self doubt like me. What was I thinking?

Many groups I spoke to didn't respond very well; in fact, one group walked out on me 15 minutes into my talk. They found me too shy and nervous, not inspirational at all. I sucked at it badly and it was humiliating. I was devastated. I had to face the fact that I was BAD at my dream career. I decided to get a therapist, hoping this would help me deal with my issues. The problem was that she just wanted me to talk about negative things from my past. I literally spent hours with her rehashing my childhood issues and my present day issues.

When that didn't seem to help, she told me to come back for more. So, I started going there three times a week, but my issues just got worse. Finally,

I quit therapy because I couldn't afford it anymore. I gave up on my dream, and got a job as a waitress again to pay the bills. At the time, it seemed like the sensible thing to do, but inside I felt like my life had hit rock bottom.

About six months later, I met someone who, today, would be called an executive performance coach. At the time, she had an eclectic blend of unusual training. She had tools for breaking you free of limiting thoughts at the subconscious level. With her, I no longer had to rehash negative things from my past, but instead I was encouraged to let all those fall away so my natural creative brilliance could shine forth. This was a much more effective model for helping a person like me to succeed.

That was the beginning of a big turn-around for me. I realized that I'd been sabotaging my own success by worrying about failing, and I was attracting what I didn't want. With her help, I was imagining succeeding. Every day, I focused on what I wanted, in lots of vivid detail. Then, eventually, I magnetized more of what I wanted – to be more confident, a better speaker, an inspirational leader, and to be more financially abundant.

That focus actually changed the way my brain processed life. Instead of problems, I saw opportunities. Instead of resisting doing the work to get better, I looked forward to it. I was like a new person. For example, I got better reviews at my summer public speaking job. I also had the courage to ask the owner of the company, Matt, to help me get better, which made a massive difference.

Then, I joined a business incubator for people under thirty, so I could run my own business. I took training to become an expert in team leadership and community building. I learned how to run a business, how to do sales and marketing, and how to manage cash flow. I got involved in the whole meetings' industry, and joined masterminds of other people in my field. I hired a speaking coach to improve my material and delivery. I studied adult education. I learned Educational Kinesiology so I could heal from dyslexia. I took assertiveness and self esteem building classes so I could be more confident. I took negotiation and conflict resolution training so that I could be a better communicator.

Naturally, my business, relationships and income started to increase. I hadn't been doing any of those things before, so no wonder I wasn't doing very well. I was then able to quit the waitressing job. Most importantly, I kept going with the inner work, transforming the fears and doubts that kept popping up, but now I had a system for turning those around. That, by far, was the most important thing I did to turn things around. I used to think that 'inner work' was a kind of "add on" or nice thing to do when you had time. Now I saw it as a priority and vitally important to clean and protect my mind regularly.

Over the years, I studied with everyone and anyone - getting the support I needed to do this work. As time went by, I became better and better at managing my mind, entrepreneurship, sales, marketing, mastering my topic, and my craft. I had many failures and tests. The supreme ordeal for me was after five years in business, when I hit burn out. I literally couldn't work for two years. I went on disability and had to live on practically nothing while I journaled and walked in the woods. I finally saw that I was trying to be someone I wasn't. I still had my mother's voice in my head expecting me to be like her, and expecting myself to be perfect in all that I did, both of which were impossible. Upon realizing that, I was able to accept myself and my imperfections much more profoundly. That's when my energy came back.

At the same time, I saw many of my colleagues suffer. They wanted to quit or had hit burn out like I had. Some reached out to me, so I helped them. I loved helping them transform the inner doubts, impossible expectations and fears. Like me, they went from sabotaging their own success, to doing whatever it took to be their best.

After awhile I cut back on my speaking and started coaching other change leaders around the world. Leaders in organizations, who were having a hard time motivating their team, started to call me. Entrepreneurs who wanted to speak at events or create online content called. They all needed the inner game work and the outer strategies that I'd spent years honing. I loved doing that just as much as being out there speaking and leading seminars myself.

Then, I met my life partner, Dave O'Connor, who'd been on a similar journey to mine. He'd faced many challenges and setbacks but had kept going as a speaker and coach for business owners, despite it all. The key had been shifting things at the subconscious level instead of just trying to consciously *will* changes to happen. This, too, made him able to break-free of self-sabotaging habits and ultimately succeed.

When we met, both of us had been on the road, for years, speaking; and though we loved it, we also had to sacrifice a lot to live like that. It was hard to live a balanced and healthy life—being on the road 40 weeks of the year. Around that time, streaming video was coming onto the scene. This meant being able to teach our programs online and not have to leave our home if we didn't want to, and to be able to work with people face to face on video from our own home office anywhere in the world.

Today we live a life and lifestyle that years ago we both would have thought impossible. We feel so blessed to be able to winter in Hawaii, summer in Vancouver, spend quality time in Europe and still do the work that we love with a passion. But it never would have happened had we not been able to both look at our lives from the various stages of the Hero's Journey and identify exactly at what point we were on the journey.

For example, when we realized we were on the road of trials – where we encountered enemies, temptations and challenges – we were able to see everything as a test to help us build more character for the journey ahead. Whenever we reached rock bottom and felt like quitting, we knew this was the part of the hero's journey often referred to as the 'ordeal' or the 'abyss' or the 'dark night of the soul'. This is the most dangerous part of the journey because often when we're at our lowest point in life we can make our worst decisions. However, knowing that this too would pass and was just another part of the process enabled us to rewrite a more empowering MindStory and keep us moving forward towards the finish line.

Eventually, we had to expand and scale our business or risk burning out again. This was a big shift both internally and externally, but that way we could better serve far more people and did so through growing our staff and certifying other coaches in our methodology. Seeing the far-reaching effects of our work around the world helped us see that the whole ordeal, the loss, the confusion, the hard work, the victories, the losses, were all very much worth it.

RE-CONSTRUCTING YOUR HERO'S JOURNEY

Now it's your turn to rewrite your MindStory. The process of reconstructing your life in terms of a Hero's Journey is profoundly life changing. To make it easier, I took the Hero's Journey structure originally created by Joseph Campbell and shortened it for business owners and experts to create their WHY story. It's called the 5-Part Ascension Story Structure. You can use this *Often you don't know where you're going in life until you start moving towards something.* for a mission story you might put on your website, as an introduction during a speech or webinar, or what to share during an interview. You may already have a WHY story, which is great. Use this process to take it to a whole other level. You'll see the 5-part structure below and the Hero's Journey sub-structure within each section.

HOW TO CHOOSE A STARTING POINT

I suggest you choose a starting point based on when you decided to become a leader. It could have been many small decisions over time, so just pick one, like I did above with seeing Dr. Caldicott speak when I was a teenager. The truth is, you are in a leadership role a lot of the time, whether you are a solopreneur, lead a team of people, or running a huge business. Even if you are in career transition, you are leading yourself.

For example, you may be leading yourself through inner conflict, or influencing a child to do their homework, or inspiring a friend to reach for their dreams. If you're reading this book, chances are you have chosen the path of a leader. You may have made many mistakes along the way. That's normal. See if you can find your journey towards becoming a leader and growing yourself and others as leaders. This focus will have a positive effect on your forward movement, allowing you to see challenges as opportunities for growth.

WHAT IF I DON'T SEE MYSELF AS A LEADER YET?

Some people don't think of themselves as a leader because they have certain expectations in their head about what a leader is. The truth is, some leaders are very charismatic, others are quiet problem solvers, then there are the bold strategists, or amazing collaborators, and some combine all those aspects and more. The overlapping aspect is that they draw people towards them and inspire action.

WHAT IF I DOUBT MY ABILITY TO LEAD?

We believe that influencing and leadership are skills that can be learned by anyone. We are all capable of stepping up and helping, inspiring and encouraging others to achieve their goals in their own ways. All too often, however, we follow the crowd, rather than stepping out from the shadows and showing up as a leader. That choice can dramatically limit your life satisfaction.

There is no doubt that in your network there will be great leaders and you will be able to learn a lot from them. But don't doubt your own ability to become one, too. That said, you cannot lead others until you've learned to lead yourself. Great leadership begins with self-acceptance, which activates compassion as well as self-discipline. Most people think leadership is what you do on the outside, but actually it is reflected by who you are on the inside. Reconstructing the MindStory of your life will help you do that.

If you haven't finished it yet, or even started, that's ok. Write the story how it might go and include all the stages. You may need to be more general than specific in some stages, but doing this will fortify you to face the dragons along the way and achieve the final elixir.

HOMEPLAY

Now it's your turn to look back through your life and see your journey of becoming a leader. Explore where you maybe went through some of these stages in the past. You can also finish the story even if it hasn't happened yet. How do you want it to end? What's an empowering ending? Make a few notes in each of the sections. This will become your outline.

Once you have your outline, you can write it out free form, no editing. Once you get it all down, you can go back and refine it. Remember, it doesn't have to be a story of epic proportions. This is initially for you and your own personal growth. Eventually, you can then refine and multi-purpose this story to build your business and magnetize ideal clients to you.

PART 1 – SETTING THE PLATFORM

Creating Curiosity – This is where you tell your reader or listener why they should pay attention to your story. What's in it for them? It's easier to write this part once you've written out and edited the whole story. Come back to this once it's done. *In my story, it's where I'm talking about having helped hundreds of people construct their mission story, and how it can help change your self-image in powerful ways for the better. In other words, it's an example so you can better understand how to do it for yourself.*

_____

_____

The Ordinary World - This is where you, as the Hero, exist before your journey as a leader begins. It's where you are unaware of the adventures to come. It's a place of safety – a comfort zone. It's also where you show parts of who you are at the core, and your outlook on life. It helps create a connection with you as the Hero to your listeners. It makes it easier for them to identify with you and your plight. *In my story, it's where I'm a teenager going through challenges and working as a waitress.*

_____

_____

PART 2 – TILTING THE PLATFORM

The Call to Adventure - Your Hero's adventure begins when you receive a call to action as a leader. Think of when that might have been for you. It can be conflict, accident, failure, trouble, mishap, discover, or new decision. Ultimately, its what disrupts your Ordinary World and presents a challenge or quest that must be undertaken. *In my story, it was seeing Dr. Helen Caldicott speak …this one event changed my life forever.*

_____

_____

The Refusal of the Call - Although you, as the Hero, may be eager to accept the quest, at this stage you likely had fears and setbacks that needed overcoming. For example, you start seeing the problems you'll have to face to achieve your dreams. *In my case, it was discovering I was bad at my dream job and so I thought of quitting.*

_____

_____

The Meeting of the Mentor - At this crucial turning point, you, as the Hero, often need guidance. Your mentors may be false mentors or true mentors, or a combination of both. Somehow, your mentor gives you insights into how to transform doubts and fears so you have the strength and courage to begin your quest. *In my case, I found a false mentor in the therapist and a true mentor in the executive performance coach.*

The Crossing of the Threshold - You are now ready to act upon your call to leadership and can truly begin your quest. You finally cross the threshold between the world you are familiar with and that which is unfamiliar. This action signifies your commitment to your journey and whatever it may have in store for you. *In my story, it was about starting my own business and being willing to do whatever it took to be successful.*

PART 3 - CONSEQUENCES

The Road of Trials (Tests, Allies, Enemies) Now that you're finally out of your comfort zone, you'll inevitably be confronted with an ever more difficult series of challenges, yet there will also be allies who help you. *In my story, it was hitting burn out, having to change core beliefs and expectations about myself and meeting my life partner as a powerful ally.*

Approach to The Innermost Cave - The innermost cave may represent many things in your story, such as an actual location in which lies a terrible danger or an inner conflict, which up until now you had not faced. At the threshold to the innermost cave you may once again face some of the doubts and fears that surfaced upon your first call to adventure. *In my story, that was the decision to go online with our business – a huge investment of time and energy that might not pay off.*

_____

_____

Ordeal / Abyss - The Supreme Ordeal or the Abyss may be a dangerous physical test or a deep inner crisis that you must face in order to keep moving forward along your destined path. Whether it is facing your greatest fear or most deadly foe, you must draw upon all of your skills. It's about some form of "death" where you felt reborn, experiencing a metaphorical resurrection that somehow granted you greater power to fulfill your destiny. This is the high point of your story - where everything you hold dear is put on the line. If you fail, life as you know it will never be the same again. *In my story, it's when we restructured our entire business so that it was mainly online.*

_____

_____

PART 4 – GETTING BACK TO STABILITY

Reward (Seizing the Sword) - After defeating the enemy, surviving death and finally overcoming your greatest personal challenge, you may have transformed into a new state and become a stronger person. The Reward may come in many forms: an object of great importance or power, a reconciliation with an ally who helps you. Whatever the treasure, you probably had to put celebrations aside and prepare for the last leg of your journey. *In* *my story, we finally figured out how to make the online portion of our business work for us and for our clients.*

The Road Back - This stage in the Hero's journey represents a reverse echo of the Call to Adventure in which you had to cross the first threshold. Now you must return home with your reward – feeling vindicated for all your courage and efforts. But the Hero's journey is not yet over and you may still need one last push back into the Ordinary World. The moment before you finally commit to the last stage of your journey usually involves choosing between your own personal objective and that of a Higher Cause. *In my story, that's where we have now designed the life and lifestyle of our dreams, and where we're feeling our purpose making a big difference for others.*

Resurrection - This is the climax in which you must have a final dangerous encounter; one that has far-reaching effects beyond your own personal life. If you fail, others will suffer. To succeed, you need to destroy an inner or outer enemy and emerge from battle cleansed and reborn. *In my story, that was where we had to expand and scale our business, to better serve people through growing our team and certifying other coaches in our methodology around the world.*

PART 5 – NEW STATUS QUO

Return with the Elixir - This is the final stage of your journey in which you return home to your Ordinary World a changed person. Your transformation now offers a direct solution to the problems of others. The final reward is self-realization beyond your own ego and survival needs. It's a feeling of having fulfilled your destiny. *In my story, it's about seeing the far-reaching effects of our work around the world, which helped us see that the whole ordeal, the loss, the confusion, the hard work, the victories, the losses, were very much worth it.*

_____

_____

CHAPTER 11

Imprinting Good Memories

Stories are the creative conversion of life itself into a more powerful, clearer,
more meaningful experience. They are the currency of human contact.
— Robert McKee

CARLA'S STORY

Jessica came to me for coaching after an interview had gone very wrong.
She was a natural leader and people she worked with loved her. They
encouraged her to apply when a management position came up. She did
and was then invited to an interview with senior management. This meant
sitting at a table opposite a panel of five people.

Everything was going okay, until one of them asked her to talk about
her accomplishments. Her mind went blank. She started sweating and
fidgeting. Her hands trembled. She looked like a deer in the headlights.
After several awkward moments, they switched the subject and finished
the interview early. She walked out feeling humiliated.

A few days later she found out that someone else got the job. Her colleagues
were outraged. They all thought Jessica should have been chosen. She knew
it had to do with her strange breakdown in the middle of the interview.

In all my years of dealing with people about fear of interviews, I can usually trace that kind of behavior to something that happened in childhood. In Jessica's case, it all went back to one incident. She was 10 years old and came home from school with an "A" on her report card and showed her family. Her parents praised her, and her older brother and sister said nothing. Later, when her parents weren't around, they punched and kicked her, and then locked her in a closet. They mocked her for getting an 'A' and trying to get her parents' approval.

Years later, she could see that they were just jealous. She was far better academically than they were. They were good at other things that she wasn't good at, but for some reason her parents really loved this quality in their youngest daughter, and her siblings hated that. She learned to never talk about her accomplishments anymore, because literally her well-being was at stake.

She used one of our tools, entitled the *Memory Imprint Journal*, for 30 days, with this issue as a focus. In the journal you write out short stories of good things that have happened to you, your accomplishments and what you're grateful for. This helped her override a fear about herself in a positive way. She wrote about a few times when her siblings were actually supportive. This happened when they were young adults, but it helped override the childhood experience.

Secondly, she wrote memories of when she talked about her accomplishments with her boss, where she was at ease, and nothing bad happened.

The object of the *Memory Imprint Journal* is to bring those kinds of memories to the front of your mind. The third thing she did was called "a memory do-over". This is where she imagined she was 10 years old again, showed her report card to her siblings and they were ok with it. Then she wrote a "future memory" about doing an interview and having everything go well. She was confident, at ease, articulate, humble, yet inspiring to others. All of these kinds of stories are a form of mental rehearsal. They helped her release the childhood trauma and create new, empowering neural pathways.

Halfway through the month, she plucked up the courage to ask for a "do-over" of her interview for a different management job. They agreed. Together we did a role play of the interview and we videotaped it. She watched herself being centered, calm and able to articulate her accomplishments in a confident way. On the day of the interview, it went exactly as she had pictured in her various mental rehearsals. They were thrilled and gave her the job.

Since then the phobia of sharing her accomplishments is mostly gone. It's like a faraway memory that doesn't affect her performance.

IS YOUR "INNER SOIL" FERTILE ENOUGH?

There is a term in the field of psycho-cybernetics called *building resources*. Many people want to increase their level of confidence, belief, and outlook on life, but just *wanting to* doesn't actually make it happen. As we've said, you have to take consistent actions over a specific period of time to create new neural pathways. Even then, a certain percentage of people still can't change. That's because they lack the inner resources needed.

Using the metaphor of a garden, their inner soil is too acidic. There are too many rocks and weeds, so the seeds die off. If they do sprout, the plants won't survive. Many people are full of acidic thoughts, beliefs and programs about life, and it's not their fault. It's the human condition. Our society is set up in a way that keeps people locked into scarcity thinking around time, money, support, self-judgment, comparing ourselves to others, being fearful of life in general. It's in the media, advertisements, the way people talk, our education system and in messages heard from many authority figures, including our parents in many cases. We are awash in these kinds of negative mindsets.

To counteract all that is to really commit to regular practices like the ones we talk about in this book. It's like going to the gym. You need to build new muscles, to create new neural pathways and to ensure those override the bad ones. The good news is that using the tools in this book, thousands of people have reported that after just 30 days, they notice moodiness, low motivation, financial problems and even physical pain in the body all decrease significantly. And, if they stop these good habits of mind, the problems come back. It's like the weeds grow back in the garden unless you continually remove them and override them.

YOU ARE WIRED FOR NEGATIVITY

A big reason people can't achieve goals in their life is because their unconscious is a mass of negative memories constantly being reinforced. That way they never get to move on and learn. They re-traumatize themselves over and over again, often without being consciously aware it is happening.

As we mentioned before, the human mind defaults to remembering negative experiences and forgetting positive ones. Those experiences get organized in the brain in narrative form with various components such as characters, scripts, emotions, setting, plot and conflict.

The problem with this kind of mind system is that humans tend to remember many more negative experiences than positive ones, giving you the overall impression that life is dangerous and unpleasant. Whereas, if you imprinted the positive memories too, you would notice they far outweigh the negative. If you really think about it, for every one negative or challenging thing in your life, probably there are a thousand things going well. Most people, however, focus on the one in a thousand going badly.

The mind will base expectations about the future on past experiences. Therefore, if you mainly remember and reinforce negative experiences about life you will attract more negative experiences. If you imprint more positive memories, you will naturally create a better future.

If you expect a better future you are more likely to be confident, relaxed, and creative about how to deal with challenges. You will tend to see the world as a safe, pleasant, supportive and wonderful place to be. As a result, you will take more risks and be more persistent and innovative. You then tend to attract more synchronicity into your life. It has a kind of domino effect.

HOMEPLAY

MEMORY IMPRINT JOURNAL
PAGE – 5-DAY CHALLENGE

For 5 days straight do Steps 1-3 and notice how your mind starts to scan for what's good and remembers good memories. It might be hard to do at first, because you're building a new muscle. After awhile, it becomes easier.

Date: _____

Part 1 - Appreciations about yourself. Include both doing and being states. E.g. I went to the gym, I finished the report, I was patient with Kyle and his homework, and I forgave myself for being late.

Part 2 - Appreciations about life's circumstances. Include both people and life circumstances that feel good and supportive. E.g. I love my home, Annette helped me with the report, I got a tax refund.

Part 3 - Memory Imprint. Use present tense and five senses to really take yourself there in the moment. About 5-10 sentences will do.

E.g. "I am 15 years old and part of the debate team. I hear myself recite my opening words at the finals. I sound confident. I feel centered and well-rehearsed. I see the audience and they look engaged. I see the other team members. I feel relieved and happy to be part of this exciting experience. It's the end and I hear them announce our team as the winner. I'm elated and so is everyone else from our school."

To get more background and on-going support to
imprint this powerful life habit, check out the
Memory Imprint Journal - Free 5 Day Challenge here:
https://mindstoryacademy.com/#free

CHAPTER 12

Protecting and Clearing
Your Mind

*There are many things we think we should do when, in
fact, we don't really have to. Getting to the point where we
can tell the difference is a major milestone in life.*
– Elaine St. James

CARLA'S STORY

Jan, a client of mine, was a brilliant speaker and coach. She came to me because it turned out that her greatest strength had become her greatest weakness. She was a motivational speaker and coach in the area of leadership. People loved working with her. They reported that after a coaching session, they felt much better. After her speaking engagements, people walked away feeling lighter, relieved and inspired.

The problem was that she felt completely drained after most of her coaching and speaking sessions. Her greatest strength was her empathy. Many people drawn to coaching and speaking are highly empathic. They need to be, in order to be effective. Empathy is like a super power that you can use for great good. You can tap into the true needs of a coaching client and know exactly how to help him or her. You can tap into the "group mind" of an audience and know exactly what to say and how to say it. People feel connected to you and they feel you care about them.

However, if you don't know how to manage this super power, it can work against you. At a subconscious level, Jan was taking on the negative feelings of her clients and audience members, and literally trying to heal them energetically. They felt lighter and better but she felt worse. This is far more common than people realize.

As her reputation grew, more and more opportunities came to her. She didn't want to say no, because she genuinely wanted to help people, and her family needed the income. But, the more she took on, the worse she felt. That's when she started acting against her character. She started showing up late for speaking engagements and not being her best on stage. She broke confidentiality with a coaching client and it backfired on her. Soon, her speaking and coaching opportunities started to die away. She was devastated on the outside and relieved on the inside. It was a classic case of self-sabotage.

This is a common theme I hear among speakers, coaches, consultants, facilitators and practitioners. They go on a roller coaster of helping people, getting popular, sabotaging their success, getting some relief, then going back out there again once they feel better. But, at that point, they have to start from scratch all over again. This is a hard way to run a business.

Once we started working together, I was able to give her a powerful process (that I'll share here), that made a huge difference. Like many overly empathic people, it started as a childhood decision that became an unconscious program working on autopilot into her adult years.

Somehow she'd made a decision at a very young age that it was her job to heal her mother of all her pain. Her mother would often come home from work exhausted and stressed out. She was a single mother, in a low paying job, just barely making ends meet. She got pregnant young and Jan's father abandoned them. She had to give up many of her dreams to become a mother. Jan picked that up unconsciously, and somehow felt like she owed her mother. As a child, she often just sat next to her mother and held her hand whenever she was upset. Soon, her mother felt relieved, and Jan would go to bed carrying all of her mother's emotional burdens.

Once we identified this unconscious childhood agreement she had made with her mother, we were able to turn it around. Unconscious agreements like this are components of an inner MindStory that can stay on autopilot into a person's adult life. She not only lived out this agreement with her mother, but with many other people in her life after that. It became the way she felt needed in the world. It was a survival tool to keep people from abandoning her.

Realizing this, she was able to create a new agreement with herself and others. The new agreement allowed her to still be empathic with others, but with boundaries. She let go of the role of healer at the unconscious level. Instead, she called in a higher, more potent source of healing to help others. If you try to heal people to make yourself feel wanted, it actually becomes a codependent relationship both ways. It's coming from the ego. It's a short-term fix, but it ultimately disempowers both parties.

She also learned to project an energetic shield around her that allowed in good, helpful energy and repelled bad or harmful energy. Highly creative and empathic people, like Jan, often become targets for parasitic people. These are people who don't know how to tap into a higher source of energy, so they must siphon creative life force energy from others. You've probably met some people like this yourself. You spend time with them and then feel negative and drained afterwards. Some of those 'vampiric' type people were her coaching clients and some were sitting in her audience. The shield helped protect her from being siphoned in that way.

These two changes led to her feeling energized after a coaching or speaking session, instead of drained. In fact, she felt more helpful to those she served. This also allowed her to stop sabotaging her forward momentum - so her business, income and reputation could grow continuously. Five years later, she was more successful than ever, and her energy remained strong both during and after working with people. In this chapter, I'll go into more detail about what she did to turn things around, in case it's useful for you.

INTERPRETATIONS BECOME AGREEMENTS

Your interpretation of events is a lot more potent than you think. As we've mentioned, we call these MindStories. Sometimes, those interpretations become agreements between you and others that can run on autopilot and affect all aspects of your life.

People often think that external events change their life. Sometimes that's true, but mostly it's not. It's usually your interpretation that creates a change - for the good or the bad. If you look back on any major turning point in your life, chances are it was HOW you interpreted it that led to the new outcome.

For example, I worked with two men at the same company. Both were laid off at the same time. Both were the same age, and had similar backgrounds and family situations. One of them decided the layoff meant he wasn't a valuable member of the team, so he intended to find a job, any job, quickly. He got a similar job, but it paid less. Three years later, he got laid off again. The other man decided the layoff meant it was a sign he should start his own business. He used his severance package and some savings to tide him over until he was profitable as a consultant. Three years later, he was making double what he made in his last job, with no boss to report to, and he was able to work from home and had freedom around his working hours. Same external situation, different interpretation, that led to two totally different outcomes.

Let's take the example of Jan. She interpreted that her mother's unhappiness at work was her fault. Was it really her fault? Her mother's choices and her interpretation of her life situation mostly led to her negative feelings. Not her child, Jan. However, when you're a child, you don't have that level of discernment.

People who can change their interpretations of events, and therefore change their agreements, can entirely change their life for the better. You'll see an example of how to do that below, in the next section.

HOMEPLAY

ENERGETIC SHIELDING

An energetic shield can protect you from harm, from taking on bad energy, and from anyone who might drain your energy. It can also nourish you and connect you more deeply, to a higher source of wisdom. Once connected, you can also break free from unconscious agreements that are harming you much more easily.

For example, I remember once creating a small garden. It was on an island in the Pacific Northwest that was overrun with deer. I was proud of myself for learning how to till the ground, fertilize it, plant the seeds, water them, and ensure they got the right amount of sunshine. After months of work, and hundreds of dollars, my garden finally bloomed. I was harvesting salad ingredients and sharing produce with neighbors. I'd done all the right things except for just one. I didn't realize about the huge deer population on the island. One morning, I came out to find they had eaten everything in my garden and trampled it all down. My neighbor then showed me how to erect a deer fence.

This energetic field is a kind of "deer fence", which you need because others can consume your life force energy if you aren't careful. I see so many highly talented people do all the right things to till, fertilize, plant and water their creative projects only to find something unexpected consuming and destroying it. It's the kind of thing that should be taught in schools. It's such an important life skill.

WHAT AN ENERGETIC SHIELD CAN DO

In order to shield yourself, it usually requires a good, strong, clear connection to a higher source of wisdom. This is like a trusted advisor within that can help you find a more constructive perspective on life, that can dismantle an old agreement, and help you make good decisions, find clarity, nourish and protect you.

That connection is going to be called different things for different people, depending on your values and how you view life. You might call it the Great Creator, God, your guides, your team, Higher Power, or just connecting into your highest brain capacity. Whatever resonates with you. You've probably had days when you feel wise, at peace, highly creative and insightful. That's the kind of connection I'm talking about. Most of us go in and out of having that connection. The more you can maintain it, the better your life becomes.

WHAT THE ENERGETIC SHIELD IS LIKE

There are many types of energetic shields you could erect. Different types work for different people. You can also have several different shields for different purposes. In this chapter, you'll learn about one that I call The Aqua Portal Shield. Maybe you've seen those documentaries with pods underwater that researchers use. The pods protect the researchers against the intense pressure of the underwater environment, and from any predators down there. The air is good inside the pod. There are instruments on the dashboard. You can see out the window as to what's coming. Basically, it allows you to travel in a foreign environment and stay healthy and able to do your work. That's what this Aqua Portal Shield will do for you.

To erect this energetic shield, you just imagine a sphere coming down around you. It starts at the top of your head about three feet above your head, and goes down to a foot below you. It's like a bubble, but it can change shape depending on whether you're sitting or standing. There's a lower grounding cord from the bottom of the shield going all the way down to the center of the earth. Then, there's an upper grounding cord going up to the center of the galaxy. So you're both grounded below, and you're also connected above. Both connections should feel grounding, supportive and nourishing.

CLEARING NEGATIVE ENERGY

Many people visualize their Aqua Portal Shield first thing in the morning, before they start their work, and last thing before going to sleep. It shields them from getting drained of energy, helps clear unwanted energy, and revitalizes them. Just as you would shower or take out the garbage regularly, you need to clear your energy system regularly. Otherwise, it gets bogged down with pollutants that can make you unhealthy. Most people are walking around with very polluted energy systems. The good news is that it doesn't cost anything, hardly takes any time, and works simply via your intention and imagination. The more you believe it works, the better it works.

To clear yourself, imagine you're inside the portal, just floating there. Then, imagine aqua-marine colored water washing through you and the portal. Say these words, "Please clear away any pollutants, toxins, stagnant energy, negative energy, any energy siphons, any agreements or vows I've made that no longer serve me." Then, just imagine those being washed away, going down the lower feedline, and going back to the earth for recycling.

Is there a device yet that measures how it works? No, but maybe that's coming in the future. Your intention and imagination are a lot stronger than you think, and people don't use them properly. They let others hijack their intentions or they use their imaginations to worry. What you focus on grows. It's like wishing for a thing that you don't want. Even if you're skeptical that this could work, there are no bad side effects that we've encountered. It doesn't hurt to take one minute a day to just do this, to set your shield and clear off the negative energy. It's better than not doing it, and most people report feeling better after they have done it. You'll notice the difference as you become stronger and stronger with it. Try it and see for yourself.

SHORTCUT

After you've done this a few times, you can just say, "Shield up," and you can create a physical anchor, like putting your thumb, index finger and middle finger together with both hands. Then just say, "Clearing." Next, make a wiping action with your hand, like you're wiping a steamed-up mirror in the bathroom. After you've done it enough times, it can happen quickly and easily. For the next 30 days, commit to doing this for one minute, three times a day.

1. First thing in the morning
2. Before you work
3. Before going to bed

GETTING AN UNOBSTRUCTED CONNECTION

You want to make sure you have a clear connection. Sometimes you think you're connected to your shield and to this higher source of power, but it's being infiltrated or there's static in the way. Let's use the metaphor of a bridge line. Say you've dialed into a bridge line for a teleconference. There's a number that you call with a password. On this bridge line, you want to talk with your trusted advisor. You just want it to be the two of you, and you want to make sure it's the right person, and that you can hear each other well. The problem is that someone else gets onto the line, or there's static, or the line drops. This can happen when connecting to your shield.

If you've had an on-going practice of tapping into this Higher connection, you probably know about this phenomenon. It's not often talked about but it's highly important. You have to ensure the shield doesn't have leaks. Create a clear intention about connecting to this inner trusted advisor, and ban all other types of connection. That alone is very powerful. The trick is to feel like you're in a purified portal, with no leaks, that has strong lower grounding and upper grounding. It's where you're not lost in your mind, with looping and racing thoughts. Instead, it's that deeper, more embodied feeling of being connected into the seat of the soul. After awhile, you'll get used to when you're connected and when you're not connected to your shield. The more you do it, the more you'll reinforce it.

Section 5

ATTENTION

ATTENTION

ATTENTION is Part 5 of the AVARA Coaching Model. It's about looking at where you focus your attention on a daily basis. Is it towards disempowering and limiting thoughts, or more empowering ones? Much of modern society tempts us into distraction. All our devices, entertainment, substances, emotional dramas – all are designed to distract you from your true life purpose. Here you learn the discipline of staying focused so you can more powerfully live your highest vision.

You can start at ATTENTION in the model, especially if you have some form of DISTRACTION going on. For example, disruptions that come from outside yourself, or inner distractions such as limiting thoughts, foggy thinking, or lack of focus. You might hear yourself say something like:

"I start every day with good intentions but
find myself easily going off track."
"I can't seem to stay focused for any length of time."
"My kids seem to need so much attention right
now, I can't get anything done."

Try using the model on your own area of distraction.

Step A – Issue: What's a problem in your life? Describe the situation. No editing. We'll refer to this as your Limiting MindStory.

E.g. I want to go from 1-to-1 coaching to group coaching. I've made progress, but every time I try to work on it, something always comes along to distract me.

Step B - Facts: Now state what you wrote above as objectively as possible. Separate facts from your interpretation - no adjectives, adverbs, descriptive phrases, feelings or opinions. From an outside perspective what would everyone agree on?

E.g. Working on building a group coaching practice.

Step C – Limiting Version	Step D – Empowering Version
Now, you're going to break your MindStory down into its components parts here in the "Limiting Version" section. Then, we'll transform it in the "Empowering Version". Start by going down this first column, then go onto Step 4, in the next column	Now that you've broken your MindStory down into its components parts, we'll transform it in this "Empowering Story". Look at what you wrote in each of the parts in the left column, and create a positive version here.
1) Acceptance: What are the limiting feelings, thoughts and meanings you are giving to this situation? Express it like this *I am* (negative feeling) *because* (negative thought). *I'm making this situation mean…* (your interpretation).	**1) Acceptance:** What are more empowering feelings, thoughts and meanings you could give to the situation? Express it like this *I have chosen to be* (positive feeling) *because* (positive thought). *A better meaning I could give this situation is…*
E.g. I'm feeling distracted because of social media, my kids and my obligations to my individual coaching clients. I'm making this situation mean that I must have ADHD. Other people seem to have lots of obligations and get things done, but not me.	*E.g. I have chosen to be focused and to prioritize reorganizing my group coaching. A better meaning is that I just need to change some habits such as be accountable to a coach, turn off notifications and stay focused.*

I AM FEELING	I HAVE CHOSEN TO BE
BECAUSE	BECAUSE
I'M MAKING THIS MEAN (List all, even if they seem unlikely or silly)	A BETTER MEANING (that would feel empowering to you)
2) Vision: What is your possible future A YEAR FROM NOW if you live from this limiting MindStory? Be specific.	**2) Vision:** What is your possible future A YEAR FROM NOW if you live from this more empowering MindStory? Be specific.
E.g. I'm still exchanging my time for money doing 1-to-1 coaching. I'm overwhelmed, overtired and feel completely burnt out. I'm taking medication for my ADHD.	E.g. I have stayed focused and launched my new group coaching program. It's making a huge difference for people, and bringing me far more income for far less work. I love my life and lifestyle.

3) Action: What action or inaction is taking place? *E.g. I'm procrastinating on making the shift from my 1-to-1 coaching model to the group coaching model.*	**3) Action:** What actions could you take to achieve this empowering VISION? Anything goes. No editing. List at least 7 ideas. Then choose 1 idea and break it down to specific, small next steps in Step E below. *E.g. Get a coach to keep me focused* 1. 2. 3. 4. 5. 6. 7.
4) Reprogram: What is a recent event or experience that triggered this issue? Use present tense as if you were there now. *E.g. I put aside Saturday to work on the group coaching program. So, there I am, all set to get to work when the phone rings. It's my friend, Sophia, asking me to give her feedback on a book proposal. She's on a deadline, so I focus on that instead. By the time I'm done, the day's over.*	**4) Reprogram:** What is a similar event or experience that might happen in the near future where it's playing out in a more empowering way? Use present tense as if you were there now. *E.g. I've put aside Saturday to work on the group coaching program. I get a request for help from another friend and politely decline. I shut off my phone and all other distractions. I get a lot done. I'm feeling so good.*

| 5) **Attention**: What are the limiting beliefs here or negative Self Talk? List all, even if they seem mean-spirited, unlikely or silly.

E.g. I just feel like a leaf in the wind, with no boundaries around people. I allow others to walk all over me. I guess I'm just not a focused person and I'm not cut out for this. | 5) **Attention**: What might be your new beliefs or Self Talk from this more empowering MindStory? Start your sentence with this progressive affirmation "Every day in every way I'm..."

E.g. Every day in every way I'm becoming a master of focus and can easily achieve my high priority goals. |

Step E - Specific Next Actions: Pick one idea from your empowering ACTION section above. What are 1 to 3 specific, small, next steps to get that started? Give each a date, delegate where possible. By breaking down big goals into small steps, it makes them feel easier to accomplish.

#	Action	Who	When
Eg	*Book a discovery call with 2 possible coaches*	*Me*	*Tomorrow*
1.			
2.			
3.			

CHAPTER 13

The Inner Game of Focus

You undermine yourself when you multi-task. You really have to focus with
all your fiber, all of your heart and all of your creativity to be successful.
– Will Smith

DAVE'S STORY

Remember my presentation in front of 500 people from earlier? The MC introduced me: *We have an amazing speaker, he's going to blow your mind, yadda, yadda, yadda … Ladies and gentlemen, Mr. Dave O'Connor…*

I walked onto the stage to a thunderous round of applause. I looked out at the sea of faces. They were so silent, you could hear a pin drop. In my mind I was still hearing Colonel Amygdala saying, *"This is going to be the worst disaster ever, you'll never get another speaking opportunity after this fiasco, etc."*

Suddenly, out of the corner of my eye, I spotted a young woman, who couldn't be more than 18 or 19, looking up at me. I noticed that there was hope in her eyes. I could see fear, but I could also see hope. In a split-second, General Frontal Lobe took over and I got a download. I realized this was about being there to serve this young woman and every single person in the audience. I had been put there for a reason.

I needed to stop making it all about me and what people might think. That just wasn't fair to anybody. I was there to serve people in whatever way was best that night. Life wanted me there and I had to trust the wisdom of that. My belief is that there is an order and a sequence to everything.

In that moment, the fear vanished and something higher within spoke through me. I felt present, focused and more my authentic self than ever before. It was like my energy was filling up the entire room. I could actually see the stress melting away from people's faces and being replaced by confidence, belief and inspiration.

I ended by saying: *If we can hold onto that state of being - the drama-free notion that we are here to offer our services to each other - and that we are here to perform with grace whatever task destiny calls forth from us next, then maybe life can be a lot less overwhelming.*

I was shocked because people were jumping to their feet and giving me a standing ovation. Suddenly, they were rushing up and saying, "Wow! That was mind blowing."

Ever since then, I've found that I can choose to focus on my highest vision and listen to General Frontal Lobe, and I can choose to ignore the distractions and the noise from Colonel Amygdala and his entourage. The capacity to focus on the thoughts, feelings, actions and goals that you want to the exclusion of the opposition is the greatest super achiever secret for success that we know of, and this chapter is about how to do that.

WE LIVE IN THE AGE OF MASSIVE DISTRACTION

Much of modern society tempts us into distraction. All our devices, entertainment, notifications and substances are designed to pull us away from our true life's purpose.

You've most probably heard the saying, "Where attention goes, energy flows," and it's so true. What you may be less familiar with is that research shows that your attention is the medium through which information appears in your consciousness. The greater the attention, the more information appears in your consciousness.

Why is this important? For years, neuroscientists have maintained that we're only using about 5-10% of our mind. This means that the secret to using the other 90-95% of your mind is to increase your capacity for greater attention. The problem is, this is becoming increasingly more difficult these days.

Do you struggle, like so many others, to focus in this world full of distraction and overwhelm? I found it fun at first. I loved the constant stream of messages and notifications. It felt exciting to connect with people all over the world instantly and to know what they were up to. Over time, however, this just became more and more distracting. I started missing deadlines and procrastinating on important actions. I noticed I was becoming less creative and more agitated. Many of my clients reported the same thing.

All these distractions are draining us. They're stealing our focus and destroying our productivity. This has cost people a LOT of time, energy and money. I believe we need to take people back to the basics. Since I first started coaching people, over 20 years ago, I've always maintained that FOCUS is the most important skill you can learn in the 21st century. Focus is a key component of what you think, how you feel and whether you take an action. Your ability to focus on your goals and avoid life's distractions is critical if you want to make breakthroughs in your life.

Over the years, I have constantly modelled the most successful minds on the planet. They, too, live in a world full of distractions. Yet, they still manage to consistently take the daily actions they need to take and somehow still have fun, flow and ease in their life. Why? Because the world's most successful people know how to manage their focus and eliminate distractions. This isn't a skill that comes intuitively. It requires practice and application, which means you too can master it.

After years of in-depth study into the psychology of attention, neuroscience and peak performance, here at MindStory Academy, we have created the perfect roadmap to skyrocket people to their next level. Attention and laser-like focus are the magic keys that unlock all of it. When you have greater control over your attention, you have your mind working for you instead of against you. Focus is the enemy of mediocrity. When you increase your capacity to focus, you create a powerful force of directed energy.

Focus also allows you to tap into present moment awareness, which we cover in more detail in Chapter 14. It's the ultimate state of detachment and neutrality from which true creativity can flourish.

The moment you focus on a goal, your goal becomes a magnet pulling resources towards you. The more you can focus your energies, the more power you will generate. A loss of focus is a form of self-sabotage as we talked about in earlier chapters. When you lose focus, you lose your power. People forget that. However, if you were driving on a rainy, dark night and someone in the passenger seat was being distracting, you probably wouldn't put up with it. That's because the stakes are high. Your safety is at risk. That's how you have to think about your high priority goals in life. Remind yourself, there's a lot at stake here.

Developing rapt and sustained attention improves everything. Your awareness increases. When you go after your goals, you will have something extra kick in. Something greater within you responds when you upgrade your capacity to focus. You will achieve far more in less time and with far less effort. You'll enhance your business, your health, and your personal productivity. Focus is the secret to managing your time and energy more effectively. It's the secret to eliminating the modern enemies of productivity, such as distraction, mental fog, overwhelm and tiredness.

Mastering your focus and attention will allow you to conquer procrastination and make consistent action a pleasurable new habit. You'll improve your decision-making and critical thinking skills. You'll solve problems more quickly and more easily than ever before. You'll build your confidence and belief levels as you maximize success in every area of your life. The benefits are unlimited. In this chapter, I'll teach you some steps to get started.

FOCUS AND SOCIAL MEDIA

Most people are so easily distracted, that they never reach their full potential. I understand; I used to be the same. Social media is fantastic for promoting your business if used properly, but it is also a thief of time if you allow it to distract you.

You can improve your ability to start a task and see it through to completion by eliminating social media distractions. By being mindful, you can maintain total focus and not be lured away by the latest Facebook post from a 'friend'. I'm not saying stay away from Facebook, but I am saying to use it wisely, instead of allowing it to use you.

Remember, where you put your attention maps your destiny. Commit to developing a capacity for world-class focus.

HOMEPLAY

#1) SWITCH ON YOUR "FOCUS BRAIN"

There are 3 main brain capacities:

1. **Centering:** The ability to coordinate the top and bottom parts of the brain. This capacity is related to organization, grounding, feeling safe and non-reactive. People who are easily reactive are unbalanced in this capacity.

2. **Laterality:** The ability to coordinate the two sides of the brain. This capacity is fundamental for reading, writing, communicating and fluid body movements. People who have trouble thinking and moving at the same time, like during sports, are unbalanced in this capacity.

3. **Focus:** The ability to coordinate the back and front parts of the brain. This capacity is the ability to be detailed and *big picture*

focused at the same time. People who either 'sweat the small stuff', or who can't stay focused on the task at hand, are unbalanced in this capacity.

Strangely enough, tight muscles in the body make your Focus Capacity unbalanced. Below are three 1-minute lengthening exercises you can do to increase good focus. Also, going to a yoga or stretch class can improve your focus along with enhancing many other brain capacities.

1. **Shoulder stretch** – Grasp the muscle of your right shoulder, near the neck with your left hand, and squeeze the muscle firmly. Exhale, and turn your head to look back over your right shoulder. Now, as you inhale, return your head to the center. Then, exhale and rotate your head to the left side, to look back over your left shoulder. Do this a total of three times. Repeat using the right hand on the left shoulder.

2. **Calf stretch** – Lean against a wall and place one foot far behind you. Start with the left foot. Pump the foot up and down to loosen up the calf muscle. Alternatively, you can stand on a stair and stretch out the back of your calf that way.

3. **Hamstring stretch** – Sit on the edge of a comfy chair and stretch your legs out in front of you. Cross your legs at the ankles and then reach towards your toes. Hold the stretch for 30 seconds. Switch the way you are crossing your ankles and do it again on the other side.

#2) YOUR RELATIONSHIP WITH TECHNOLOGY

Neurotherapists have been able to track the effects of digital technology on people's brains. With the help of electro-encephalography, also known as EEG, it is possible to learn more about conditions such as depression, addiction or ADHD.

For example, focus difficulties can be due to three different causes: under-stimulation, over-stimulation or excessive challenges. Research indicates that watching too much TV leads to inertia because of under-stimulation, whereas digital media has the opposite effect. It's highly stimulating. It trains your brain to want a higher level of arousal, where you can't sustain focus on something mundane anymore. If you're under pressure from multiple sources, such as child care, work deadlines and a health challenge all at the same time, this can cause you to lose focus, as well.

Excessive use of digital technology weakens your ability to stay focused during challenges, and yet challenges often lead to the use of more digital technology. For example, if people have low level depression or anxiety, instead of turning to friends, family or normal support networks these days, they go online.

Answer these questions honestly.

1. Can you be away from digital technology for 24 hours or more without a sense of withdrawal?
2. When you feel anxious or depressed, do you go online or use TV to feel better?
3. Do you get distracted easily or agitated if you are under-stimulated, such as doing mundane activities like washing the dishes, walking, waiting in a line or driving? Do you need to have music playing or check your text messages or scroll online?

If you answered yes to any of these questions, here are a few activities to give your brain a break from constant digital technology:

1. When you first wake up in the morning, the first hour that you are alive, alert and awake – do NOT go online. Do not check your email. Do not look at social media. Don't even check your voicemail. Instead, create morning rituals that are offline, such as, meditation, exercise, or journaling.
2. Have a mind break during the day by going for a 5-10 minute walk in nature. Use this time to practice being in the now, using all the

senses. If you can go to the woods or be outside near the ocean or just in the open air looking at a beautiful vista, do that.

3. The last component is to not check your email, voice mail, texts or social media feeds at all in the last hour of your day. People are literally lying in bed and getting distracted online and they can't figure out why they aren't getting a good night's sleep.

WHAT IF'S

A final thought before we leave this chapter. A positive focus almost always has to be learned. Most people think they are positive, but upon further investigation discover they are not. How can you tell? How many negative thoughts do you have in a day versus positive ones? Consider from the moment you wake up, how does your day begin? Many people report these kinds of thoughts:

It can't be morning already; I'm so tired.
I have so much work to do today, I'll never get it all done.
I'm so frustrated that I'm not making enough income.
It's a miserable day; it's raining again.
I don't want to go to work today.
My back still aches.

I could go on, and that's just for the first few minutes in the morning!

Now is the time to change that default setting.

It's called the 3-to-1 ratio. Barbara Fredrickson, the genius of the positive psychology movement, coined the term.

Try to consciously and unconsciously generate at least three positive thoughts and feelings for every one negative thought and feeling that you have. It can help decrease negativity and increase positivity. For example, you can catch yourself and do a turnaround. Like we mentioned in Chapter 8, you can feed your brain with positive "What if" statements to counteract the negative ones.

NEGATIVE THOUGHT	POSITIVE "WHAT IF"
It can't be morning already; I'm so tired.	*What if I have a high energy day anyway?*
I have so much work to do today, I'll never get it all done.	*What if I get the most important things done anyway, and enjoy my day?*
I'm so frustrated that I'm not making enough income.	*What if I attract good income today?*
It's a miserable day; it's raining again.	*What if I enjoy the rain today?*
I don't want to go to work today.	*What if I enjoy my work today?*
My back still aches	*What if my back gets better today?*

Just remember, these kinds of thoughts will make or break your day. Do NOT under-estimate them. It's never about what's outside you; it's always about how you're thinking about it all. Clean your mind up before you start your day, just like you would have a shower or brush your teeth.

If you want your life to flourish, you'll need to generate at least a 3-to-1 ratio of positive thoughts to negative. If you generate less than 3-to-1, your efforts will likely fail.

Congratulations, you are now learning to master your focus. If you master your focus, you can control your thinking, feel better, increase your power, design your destiny and write your own ticket in life!

## CHAPTER 14

Staying in the Flow
and Being Present

The past and the future are only in your mind. True reality is in the NOW.
– Sir Nisargadatta Maharaj

CARLA'S STORY

One silent meditation retreat changed my view of reality forever. It was a Buddhist Vipassana retreat, where you sit or walk in meditation, in silence, for 5 days. The idea was to practice staying in the present moment as much as possible. I thought I'd die of boredom or agitation. I only went because several of my friends were going. And, it ended up being one of the best experiences I've ever had. After my initial resistance, I found I loved sitting in silence. I felt a huge sense of relief. I felt happy. I was released from the bondage of all the frenzied, rushing energy, of worrying about the future and looping about the past.

After the retreat, the effects permeated all aspects of my life. Strangely, I could do yoga poses that I'd never been able to do before, like touching my toes. I saw that my mind had created a lot of the tension in my body, and if I let my mind rest, my body would open up.

My listening improved. I went to visit my aging father who was hard of hearing. My habit was to sit vacantly for hours while he complained about his arthritis, the error on his bank statement, and how hard it is to find good slippers. I surprised myself by totally paying attention to him with patience and compassion. After about ten minutes of complaining, he suddenly changed tracks and started telling me fascinating and funny stories about his childhood. Then, he cranked up his hearing aid and asked about me! That hadn't happened in years.

The big test was traveling for work. I had to speak at a high profile event in Los Angeles, and I had to travel the same day as the event. The traffic was bad, the security line was long and there was a good chance I was going to miss my flight. Normally, I would be panicking. This time, however, I was calm and collected inside. In fact, I took the risk of getting out of line and asking the security guard whether I could go through the fast track line. He agreed. This allowed me to make my flight on time. Normally, I would have stayed stuck in my survival brain unable to think of solutions like this.

I even had time to buy a bag of cashews before getting on the flight. I found a place in the departure lounge and put the cashews down on a table between two seats. Then, I responded to some text messages. Now, the weird thing is, a few minutes later, the woman beside me picked up my bag of cashews, opened them and started to eat a few. I looked over at her. She smiled and offered me some.

Normally, I would've reacted and said something to her, but instead I was still in the flow of the meditation retreat. I smiled at her and took a few cashews. Then, she ate some more, then offered me more. We both sat munching my cashews, in silence, until they were all gone. Then, as we were boarding the airplane, we started chatting. I don't normally chat to people in line, but I was in an open and curious state of mind. She asked what I do and seemed very interested. Long story short, she ended up connecting me to a group who hired me not just once but many times over.

Here's the biggest irony. As I was getting settled into my seat, I opened my carry-on bag and there was my bag of cashews. She had shared HER bag of cashews with me!

Ever since that retreat experience, I've created daily habits to stay in the flow state and be as present as possible

DESPERATION VERSUS FLOW

More and more research proves that being in a state of flow is one of the greatest secrets to success in life. Nothing repels people or opportunities more than its opposite, desperation.

Flow is the mental state of operation in which you are fully immersed in whatever you are doing. You are energized, focused, with full involvement in the process of the activity. Most of us have some activities in life where this is easy to do, such as, playing a sport like tennis, or writing a blog post, or making music. The trick is to put that flow state into all tasks, no matter how mundane.

WHEN ARE YOU IN THE FLOW?

Mihaly Csikszentmihalyi, author of *Flow: The Psychology of Happiness,* says creativity is a central source of meaning in our lives. A leading researcher in positive psychology, he devoted his life to studying what makes people truly happy: *When we are involved in creativity, we feel that we are living more fully than during the rest of life.* He is the architect of the notion of flow - the creative moment when a person is completely involved in an activity for its own sake.

Csikszentmihalyi interviewed some of the most creative people in the world who experienced this flow state. People who are at the top of their game, such as artists, scientists, composers, dancers and poets, describe an effortless, spontaneous, timeless feeling – like entering a doorway into another realm. Albert Einstein gave a similar explanation to the forces of relativity.

It happens in other activities. For instance, leading athletes in the world talk about the flow experience as being that moment when all the training, all the preparation and all the pain come together to deliver the perfect performance. Top achievers in the world tend to experience that state quite often.

HOW TO FEEL HAPPY

One of the fundamental questions that almost everyone asks us is how to feel happier. The way that most people go about being happier is they try to go out into the world and achieve something external in their environment.

If you buy that car, if you lose weight, if you get out of debt, if you make a few million, if your business becomes a success, if you find the perfect relationship, then you'll be happy. Your mind will continue to search for something outside of itself to gain happiness and, ironically, this brings you into the cycle of unhappiness. The paradox is that even if you get what you want you'll often snap back to being unhappy because there's some other goal you now want that's out of reach.

It's easy to get burned and exhausted living that way, because that's not how the world works. As we've discussed many times in this book, your thinking is the source of your life experience, and as long as you don't understand this, you will blame external circumstances and factors over which you have no control.

Amazingly, if you don't understand how your mind works, you won't be happy no matter how wonderful your circumstances are. That is because you will feed the negative thoughts that then produce the negative feelings.

You'll never find happiness on the other end of a goal because it's generated inside of you. The trick is to make your happiness independent of external circumstances.

You can decide to be happy if you have a car...or not.

You can decide to love your body if you lose weight... or not.

You can decide to be compassionate with yourself if you get out of debt...
or not.

You can decide to have a great life if you make a few million... or not.

You can decide to feel good about life if you have a successful business...
or not.

You can decide to be happy if you find the perfect relationship... or not.

Consider the possibility that you don't have to be controlled by what happens outside you. What a relief! You can simply be happy even in circumstances that are less than perfect. When the negativity and self-judgment fall away, you will lighten up and be much more fun to be around.

We highly recommend that you break that illusion, and not just intellectually, but to know it in your heart. If you don't, then your search for external happiness will most definitely bring you unhappiness.

Happiness occurs when you allow your mind to focus on good thoughts, empowering meanings of life events, which lead to good feelings, which lead to inspired actions, which reprogram you for more good things. Only in a good feeling state can new answers emerge to solve old problems.

Happiness is a state of flow that will allow you to see old problems in new and creative ways and allow you to make better decisions leading to better results. To enter the flow state, you need to cultivate mental relaxation. Most people are highly tense and agitated a lot of the time. The good news is that you can train yourself to be more relaxed, at peace and happy by your choice of thoughts and interpretations. Remember, you are always only one thought away from a good feeling.

WHY THE FLOW STATE MAKES YOU MAGNETIC

The flow state is the starting point for being charismatic. People often think charisma is just something you are either born with or not. Yet, if you think about it, you probably have days when you feel charismatic, or where you're magnetizing good experiences. People are responding positively to you.

Then, other days, it seems like the opposite is happening. Your day is full of complaints, issues, glitches and barriers. We're not saying you are fully responsible for what life brings. The world around us is a co-creative experience, and sometimes negative experiences are a blessing in disguise.

That said, you DO contribute to how the world shows up for you. Most people operate in a non-charismatic way. They are rushing through activities and feeling frustrated because they haven't reached their goals yet. This state actually repels their goals and invites negative interactions.

HOMEPLAY

Training your mind to be more present is one of the most effective ways to access the flow. The Buddhists call this *walking the middle path*. If something goes badly, you take the learnings and then go back to a neutral state. If something fantastic happens, you celebrate and feel gratitude, then go back to the neutral state. You then don't need to feel like a ship without a rudder, where you feel like a victim to the ups and downs of life. You experience them, but you go back to neutral very quickly.

#1 – BEING PRESENT IN NATURE:

Practice present moment awareness by going out into nature. This is the easiest way to start. Use your 5 senses to observe your surroundings. Try to stay with the experience and not let your mind run off and think of something else. Simply focus your awareness on the present moment, and notice what you see, hear, feel-physical, feel-emotional, smell, taste.

For example, *I see an oak tree, I hear the wind blowing through the leaves, I feel the grass under my feet, I feel at peace, I smell the Hyacinth flowers, I taste the crisp spring air.*

At first, this takes discipline; but, as you feel the rewards of peace and contentment, it will motivate you to continue this habit.

I see: _____

I hear: _____

I feel physically: _____

I feel emotionally: _____

I smell: _____

I taste: _____

#2 – BEING PRESENT WHEN YOU'RE WAITING:

There are times throughout your day when you have to wait. You're in an elevator, stuck in traffic, or in a line. Those are times that many people get frustrated and impatient, especially if you're dealing with a deadline. This state of mind raises your stress hormones, distracts your mind into the future, and makes you a magnet for negativity. To help you break free of that state, take one minute to do this activity. Again, state what you see, hear, feel emotionally, feel physically, smell and taste.

For example, I was stuck in traffic recently, and here's what I said out loud to myself. *I see the red car in front of me. I hear the hum of the car engine.*

I feel tension in my jaw. I feel the car seat against my back. I smell and taste my cup of tea.

That forced my focus into the present moment and calmed me down. If I could see my brain scan as I did this, the energy would no longer be clustered in the survival brain, but dispersed back into the high brain functions of the neo-cortex. Try it yourself the next time you're feeling impatient.

I see: _____

I hear: _____

I feel physically: _____

I feel emotionally: _____

I smell: _____

I taste: _____

#3 – CHANGE YOUR RELATIONSHIP WITH TIME:

Some people unconsciously create these rushing experiences because they are addicted to the stress hormones. They leave late for a meeting so that they have to rush to get there. When I first discovered this addiction to cortisol, I started creating new habits of being on time.

For example, hours before leaving, I would put my bag at the door with everything I would need for my meeting; all my notes, water, directions, coat and shoes ready to go. My outfit would be picked out and be lying on my bed. I would leave an extra 15 minutes for traffic and glitches.

At first, it was uncomfortable to NOT be rushing, and to actually arrive early for a meeting. I heard inner thoughts such as, "This is a waste of time" or "I could have answered 3 more emails." Then, I changed my thoughts to, "It's so nice to not be rushing" or "I love getting to enjoy the whole journey to where I'm going."

List at least 3 new habits you could create in order to be on time for things.

HABIT #1 _____

HABIT #2 _____

HABIT #3 _____

CHAPTER 15

Life wants You to Win

*As a single footstep will not make a path on the earth, so a single thought
will not make a pathway in the mind. To make a deep physical path,
we walk again and again. To make a deep mental path, we must think
over and over the kind of thoughts we wish to dominate our lives.*
– Henry David Thoreau

DAVE'S STORY

It was 2001 and I had come to a crossroads in my career. I was working for someone else. I knew I was destined for bigger things and that I needed to be my own boss to do that. I decided to attend a personal development seminar in London. It was just an introductory evening. There were two thousand people there! I remember walking into a huge ballroom. The speaker wasn't on stage yet. He was at the back of the room coordinating with the sound technician. I caught his eye for a moment and he nodded to me.

There was a video playing before he got on stage. It was introducing the speaker's background. It was all very enthralling to me. I ended up staying for the whole weekend. Being there in that room rekindled a vision I had had since my teens. I saw myself speaking on huge stages helping people overcome limiting beliefs and being able to live their dreams. For years, however, I had had a huge fear of public speaking and so this dream had seemed far away for a long time.

Luckily, over the years, I had successfully failed forward and overcome that fear; and, now, I had actually become quite a good speaker within the company I was working for. I said to myself, "I've been waiting for this opportunity my whole life. THIS is what I'm meant to do! To speak in front of thousands of people, all over the world, and make a huge difference to people's ability to believe in themselves." I had never been more excited. Right there and then, I made the decision to play at the highest level, to achieve my wildest dreams, to make my vision a reality and to commit to living my greatest life.

I was essentially agreeing to go my own hero's journey, a journey I had been avoiding for many years. Along my destined path, I encountered many enemies, obstacles and challenges. But I prevailed. And, now, Carla and I have had more success than we ever thought possible, and we're very appreciative of everyone who has helped us get there.

In fact, each day that I sit back and review my life, I am humbled by our success. I am in awe of what life has done for us. It's profoundly satisfying to live a life on purpose; to aim toward success and hit it. We can all do this in our own way.

More than reaching our goals, it's who we've grown into that excites us the most. Through the MindStory AVARA model, we've had tremendous success because of the ability to free our minds and find sovereignty of spirit, and to help others do the same. We feel free in terms of our relationship with our own selves and our willingness to overcome great obstacles, to get used to leaving our comfort zone, to generate any emotion and feel like we've attained a level of mindset and maturity that helps us get through all of the discomfort that we experience because our goals are so big.

YOUR PATH TO MASTERY

If you are still reading the book at this point, congratulations! You obviously already have a good level of focus and motivation to succeed, which will help you become even better. You are now in the home stretch, and if you have been applying the principles and working through the exercises you should be well on your way to a more positive, purposeful, productive life.

Following the principles in this book every day is in itself an empowering habit and gives you a jumpstart on most people in this world who never take the time to develop mastery over their own minds. Just by reading this far, you've most likely gained greater control of your thoughts and emotions while building new positive habits.

Hopefully, you have a clearer vision now and are taking high leveraged actions more consistently. You have learned to focus on what you want as opposed to what you don't want. You know how to better deal with obstacles and understand that the path to success is paved with failure.

Imagine how exciting and fulfilling your life will be if you continue to apply these principles every day. What kind of future becomes possible when you master even a few of the concepts in this book? Imagine the results you could have over the next year and the impact your offerings could have in the world. Continue to practice the principles in this book and you will create the life and lifestyle you deserve.

You will increase your mental strength and improve your health and well-being. You will have more confidence, knowing that you are on the right path and moving towards the next level of your vision. This will add to your enjoyment of the journey and will enhance your understanding of your own true nature.

WHAT IF MY GOALS AREN'T HAPPENING?

If you find yourself disillusioned or disappointed because your goals haven't been met as quickly as you wanted, you need to become like a detective. There are many possible reasons.

1. **INCORRECT DATE:** Maybe you got the date wrong, the timing wasn't quite right – so what? It's simply life giving you the feedback that you need to dig deeper and work on your inner game a bit

more. Just have the courage to move on and set a new date for attaining the goal. Ask life for the wisdom to do better so you can manifest it, knowing it's the journey of getting there that's as important as the goal itself.

2. **WRONG GOAL:** Maybe in the process of going after your goal, you realized it was off purpose for you. Sometimes, you don't know until you try. Then, you simply "course correct" and reset your sails for a new horizon.

3. **YOU'RE TOO ATTACHED**: Maybe you're too attached to the outcome. If you want something very badly, you actually block it from coming about. It's an interesting paradox. The trick is to clearly state your goal with specificity, focus on it, turnaround the doubts and fears, then let it go, deciding to be happy whether or not it comes into your life.

These principles work. You have your inspired outcomes; you are working towards your vision. What we never know is how long it will take to achieve our goals. Is it weeks, months or years? The Universe has a sense of timing that we can never comprehend with our conscious mind.

Remember, there's a gestation period from the time you conceive your goal, to the time you believe it and achieve it.

It is important to put a date on your goals, because, without one, it's just a dream. A deadline gives you a focus and increases your enthusiasm. You are inspired to take more action and work harder if the clock is ticking. But, a date is still only a best guess, so don't give up if your timing is off.

When things don't work out exactly as we want, that's when the self-doubt creeps back in. When that happens, keep going back to this inner work and believe stronger.

WHY SUCCESS IS NOT A STRAIGHT LINE

Most people seem to have a subconscious, or even a conscious expectation that the path from A (our vision) to B (vision becomes reality) should be a straight line. In reality, it rarely is. Life is, more often than not, a zigzag journey that zips all over the place. Remember that your higher self, the inner wisdom that you keep infusing with your vision, your goals and your positive energy are always working for you and know infinitely more than you will ever understand.

The linear, logical part of you will always crave instant results and evidence of success. You must learn to trust your inner power and believe that however impossible it might seem, every step is carrying you towards your vision – even when it looks at times as if you're taking a step backwards!

"Vision without action is merely a dream. Action without vision just passes the time. Vision with action can change the world."
— Joel A. Barker

WHY COMMIT TO A PATH OF MASTERY?

Most people consciously or subconsciously commit to a path of mediocrity. They decide: *I'll just do enough to survive, to not be fired, to make just barely enough to live on, to play small, to not rock the boat, to not challenge the status quo, to not break out of my comfort zone, to make sure people approve of everything I do.*

Those MindStories keep people enslaved. No one, at the core of their true self, wants to be enslaved in this way. Nor should they be. We believe you're meant to be the best version of yourself, to achieve mastery. That said, the path there is like the Hero's Journey that is fraught with discomfort, so it's easy to give up on yourself. However, if you commit to the Path of Mastery, then that becomes your guiding light. The Universe conspires to then support you, especially when things get tough.

ALLOW THE UNIVERSE TO HELP YOU

What we discovered was that the Universe often has a better plan, one that is often beyond our wildest dreams. Maybe you've noticed that Life can bring things to you in mysterious and unexpected ways. It's like when you are ready, Providence moves too and the magic happens. Staying connected to your higher mind helps dramatically. Trying to do it all alone with your conscious mind running the show, will prove to be very difficult or impossible. Allow a true, straight mental path and connection to your unconscious mind to lead, guide, teach and show you the way.

The problem is we forget to listen; or we let the connection get interrupted, or we misinterpret the message. Apprentice yourself to creating a strong, clear, true connection. That's why we are so keen on helping you transcend worry, stress and negativity, because those states block your connection to your higher power. Many people block the connection because of negative past experiences. They decide there is no higher power, that Life is meaningless, or that Life is against them. You may need to heal that relationship first. That's why re-interpreting the meaning you've given to past experiences can be one of the most important things you do. Often the hardest experiences in life give you the greatest gifts, if you can let the learning in. That's when you can rebuild trust with this Higher Power, and let The Universe help you again.

ENJOY THE JOURNEY

If all the right ingredients are in place, success will flow as a natural result. It won't seem difficult or forced, but rather that joyful feeling of right time, right place.

For many people, the anticipation of their dreams coming true can be better than their dreams actually coming true. Do you remember the anticipation of going on that special vacation? Then it didn't match your expectations? It doesn't matter because the anticipation created so much positive emotion that it made the journey a lot more fun.

When you go after success, let yourself feel the positive feelings of achievement now. As soon as you set the intention and you start believing in the possibility, you don't even have to achieve it to enjoy it. Isn't that interesting? Enjoying all your goals ahead of time is the key. As we've said, the paradox is to set outrageous goals AND be happy at the same time with what you have now.

Staying in a perpetual state of frustration because you haven't reached your goal defeats the purpose of life. Find a way to love the process. The true purpose of any goal is the journey of growing into the person who is worthy of the goal. That's why you can't hate your way to success. You can't stress your way to freedom. If you do, you'll either block your success or reach the top and hate the view.

Continually ask yourself - How can I enjoy the journey towards my goals and dreams? That's the only question that matters; because, as soon as you set a goal, if you feel yourself tightening up, you're doing it incorrectly.

Often, you hear people throwing their lives away to create their business. They do it at the expense of their health, at the expense of their family and friends. That's a trap. As soon as you stop loving it, you have inner work to do to realign yourself with the vision. Your present is nothing more than a reflection of your past thinking, choices and actions. It doesn't have to be anything to do with who you are or where you are going.

This book is not a one-time program. It is a blueprint for achievement, personal evolution and success. It is a formula you can use to bring about any goal, and it can be used again and again. In fact, we invite you to make it part of your on-going development.

HOMEPLAY

NEW SOLUTIONS BRAINSTORM WORKSHEET°

INSTRUCTIONS: Choosing THE PATH OF MASTERY usually involves "thinking outside the box." The human mind often needs to be "tricked" into breaking out of old patterns. One way is to state your issue and then your ideal outcome below. Then, in Part 1, fill up both columns with ideas. Any idea goes. Then switch to Part 2, where you choose the best 1-3 ideas and actionize them. Use this worksheet to help you get there.

ISSUE: _____

IDEAL OUTCOME: _____

Part 1 – What's Possible (no editing, anything goes)			
#	Idea	#	Idea
1		6	
2		7	
3		8	
4		9	
5		10	

Part 2 – Choose your top 3	1st small step. Keep it simple	Who will start it?	By what date?

CONCLUSION

Specific Next Actions

At the end of each AVARA Model you've been seeing this:

Step 5 - Specific Next Actions: What are at least 3 actions you could take to ensure this new MindStory creates positive results in your life? Give them each a date, delegate where possible. Break down big goals into small steps so that they feel easier to accomplish.

#	Action	Who	When
1.			
2.			
3.			

WHY 3 SMALL ACTIONS?

You don't always need to list three. It can be just one or two. But always write down and take at least one action step towards your goal. It's true that sometimes the issue you're turning around is more about focusing on a "being" state, rather than on a "doing" state. For example, making a strong decision, would be a "being" state action. A limiting MindStory will return if you don't keep the empowering MindStory front of mind and take consistent, small action steps.

As a suggestion, you can add these kinds of small actions to improve a "being" state:

#	Action	Who	When
Eg	*Put the "Every day in every way..." affirmation on my fridge*	Me	Today
Eg	*Re-read the empowering Mindstory column every day for 21 days*	Me	Daily for 21 days
1.			
2.			
3.			

HOW IS THE ACTION SECTION OF THE MODEL DIFFERENT FROM THE "SPECIFIC NEXT ACTIONS"?

In the "Limiting Version" column you'll explore **Action** in terms of how certain MindStories lead to certain actions or inactions. Often you don't realize how your MindStories cause your actions and therefore your results in life. This realization can be a huge motivator to change.

For example, procrastination about writing a book is often caused by fear of failure. This realization can help you transform procrastination once and for all because you're addressing it at the root cause. What most people do is think that procrastination is caused by laziness and therefore they try to change it via will power alone.

For example, Nadia was trying to write a book, and thought she was just being lazy. That activated an unresolved issue between her "inner parent" and "inner child." The inner parent would bully the inner child into taking action, pushing her hard and spending days overworking, writing sixteen hours a day. Then, inevitably, the pendulum would swing in the opposite direction. The inner child would rebel and refuse to do anything for weeks afterwards, overindulging in food, shopping and movies. This inconsistency with her work, made it hard for her to progress with the book. It was a case of *one step forward and two steps back.*

In the "Empowering Version" of the Action Section, it helped Nadia see that empowering MindStories led to better actions and inactions. Once she turned around a fear of failure, she realized, "I'll likely stop doing distracting activities like shopping and start focusing on the book again in more consistent and balanced ways." In other words, the Action sections in Step C and D are about broad, overall actions or inactions.

In contrast, the "Specific Next Actions" are designed to break down what you wrote in the Empowering Action section. "Working on the book consistently and in balanced ways" is then broken down into easy-to-implement, small steps. For example:

1. Schedule writing time in calendar
2. Brainstorm on Chapter 6 content
3. Outline Chapter 6
4. Write Chapter 6
5. Edit Chapter 6

That way, it felt easy for her to get started. A goal like "finish the book" felt overwhelming, but "Add writing time into calendar" would take 5 minutes, and she could get started now. Then she could tick it off, feel a sense of accomplishment and move on to the next thing. Most people don't break down big goals into smaller steps and so stay in the overwhelmed state of mind.

Commonly Asked Questions

These are questions that our clients and coaching certification students often encounter. We thought they'd be helpful for you.

1. **Can you just change your actions, and then your MindStory changes?**

   Yes. We have seen it work, but that is definitely more challenging. At times, it's necessary to 'feel the fear and do it anyway.' However, it is much easier to transform a limiting MindStory into an empowering one, and then you'll naturally find yourself eager to take empowered actions. If you try to take the empowered action while you still have a limiting MindStory, it can create inner conflict as discussed previously with Nadia who was trying to write a book. But yes, it can be done. Just make sure you then go back and change the limiting MindStory or your new results will only be temporary.

2. **I find it hard to admit the "meaning" I'm giving to an issue in my life. How can I get past this?**

   Ask yourself why it is hard to admit that you're giving that meaning to your issue. This question will reveal a deeper meaning that can help you break free. Remember, you don't have to admit these thoughts to anyone but yourself. Some of us have a hard time admitting our interpretations because we judge ourselves for doing that. This serves no purpose and has no upside. Try to be curious and compassionate with yourself when doing this work.

Most people do this. There is a reason why you think the way you do, and finding that reason can free you. It's OK. It's also OK to change your thoughts now. You can give yourself permission.

3. **What if I can't figure out what I am feeling?**

    Breathe. Sit still. There may be many different feelings going on at the same time. Ask yourself which is the most dominant just to get a starting point. Start with the basic ones like sadness, agitation, frustration, anxiety. You can use the acronym SAFA, to remember them. You can often link other emotions back to these. For example, grief, disharmony, anger, fear - are related to these. This process is more an art than a science. You don't have to be too specific for this to work. If you feel negatively, it is worth doing the work to find the thought causing it.

    The more you get in touch with your body and the different vibrational frequencies that different thoughts cause, the more you will be able to identify and name your feelings more specifically, and then once you do that, you can more easily identify the subconscious thought looping in the background.

4. **Do thoughts always cause my feelings? Don't feelings just overcome you sometimes?**

    Yes, in the vast majority of cases your thoughts will cause your feelings. That said, there are three levels of feelings. One level is caused by physical sensations. For example, if you were to peer over the edge of a tall building to the ground below it can cause an involuntary feeling of fear. It's a reaction that moves straight from the survival brain into the nervous system of the body, without going through the brain.

    The second level is that soon after we process the experience through the brain, we think a thought that either intensifies the fear ("I could fall and die!") or lessens the fear ("I'm safe up here. What an amazing view!").

The third level is from looping programs in the subconscious we call "Core Beliefs."

You may have a core belief regarding a fear of heights that got lodged in there from a bad experience that has not been resolved. It's still stored in the trauma center of the brain, causing an overreaction when in a similar situation. You may instead have a core belief regarding being comfortable with heights, causing you to view the situation from a more positive perspective. For the sake of this work, the most important distinction is in understanding that our thoughts and core beliefs—not external circumstances or other people—cause our feelings. Even with involuntary physical reactions, the feeling would then be intensified or lessened by our thoughts and core beliefs.

5. **Is it always important to write down your issue and break it down on paper?**

Not always, but in the beginning, we recommend you write it all down. By getting your thoughts on paper, it makes it much easier. The physical act of doing this helps create more empowering neural pathways in your subconscious. Use paper, napkins, Word processor, whatever you have at hand. Start this way with the AVARA model – Acceptance, Vision, Action, Reprogram and Attention

LIMITING
A
V
A
R
A

EMPOWERING

A

V

A

R

A

This can be done anywhere, anytime in only a few minutes. It stops the looping and allows you to see it all more clearly. It activates what's called the Witness Consciousness, which is a more whole brain way of thinking (versus survival brain thinking). Once you get better at it, you might be able to do it quickly in your head, but for painful thoughts, we recommend that you still write out and complete the entire model.

6. **I'm not totally sold on the idea that my thoughts cause my feelings. My teenager really does say negative things to me—I don't just "think" she does.**

It is never your teenager. You can't outsource your feelings. Her actions are caused by her feelings and her thoughts cause her feelings, not yours. Everything your daughter says is neutral. You get to choose whether or not to make it negative with your own thinking. What you think about what your daughter says is what causes your feelings. If you believe her or think she is disrespecting you or if you think she should be behaving in a way that is different from reality, you will feel pain.

No one causes your feelings but you. We know it's hard to break the habit of thinking, "She hurt my feelings," but that thought is always a lie. You hurt your own feelings each and every time.

Now, again, this is not condoning her behavior or suggesting you just let her walk all over you. Just consider the idea that you are choosing to believe what she says, so you hurt your own feelings. Once you see that, you can break free of getting triggered by what she says or does. Then you are in a better position to negotiate healthy boundaries. If you try to change the way she acts, from a triggered state, then you'll just escalate the situation.

7. **How do I write out just the facts of the issue without my interpretation? And why is that important?**

When you write out your MindStory at the beginning of the AVARA model process, it's a chance to get it all down unedited. It's important that you don't judge yourself, or edit what you write. Most people mix facts, interpretations, beliefs and feelings together. The AVARA model guides you to break it down into its component parts, so you can then reconstruct your MindStory in a more empowering way.

For example, a MINDSTORY versus FACTS would be "My landlord entered my apartment without my consent, then changed my faucet. Now it doesn't work with my new water purifier that cost me $2000. He won't change it back to a faucet that works with my system. He has no respect for me and my situation."

The same situation listed just as the FACTS would be: "My landlord changed my faucet and now it doesn't work with my water purification system."

Can you see how unemotional that second one is? This was important because upon further investigation the landlord did have permission to enter the suite. It turned out that the faucet was an upgrade, since the old one was leaking and causing damage. One adaptor solved her problem, which the landlord willingly provided for her, once she approached him in an "untriggered" state. The AVARA model helped her get there.

8. **How do I deal with frustration and disappointment when my life circumstances don't match my vision?**

What helps is to change an expectation to a preference. For example, a client worked hard on a proposal for funding and was assured by a colleague that she had a very high chance of it being accepted. Instead, it got rejected. She was very disappointed and frustrated because she complexly expected to get it. Upon doing the AVARA model she realized she was making the rejection mean that Life was against her, that she was bad at writing proposals, that her kind of business will never get funding. Once she changed her thought about the situation to "I would have preferred to receive it", instead of "I should have received it", then the frustration and disappointment dissipated. A better meaning she chose was that maybe Life was supporting her, and that particular grant money might send her in the wrong direction, that the experience taught her a lot about writing proposals, that her kind of business could still get funding from other sources. Those thoughts then helped re-ignite her creative energy to get other sources of funding. In the end, she got a business loan which gave her far more freedom to run her business.

9. **Can I use the AVARA Model to help me manifest a goal versus sort out an issue? For example, to move to another country.**

Yes, just start with the goal, and then explore both your limiting MindStories and empowering ones. Usually when you set a goal, it tends to trigger obstacles in your own mind, many of which are subconscious. This process helps bring them to the surface so you can examine how you want to proceed. Then choose which actions will help you get there. If you set a goal without doing a process like this, the subconscious obstacles can sabotage your forward movement.

10. **In the limiting MindStory column, I notice that what I write in ACCEPTANCE about "what I'm making this mean" is similar to the Self Talk I write about in ATTENTION?**

That's often the case, and that's okay. In ATTENTION, you're also going to uncover the deeper, limiting belief driving the Self Talk. It's just coming at the underlying interpretations and thoughts from another angle.

11. **What if I can't yet believe what I wrote in the empowering column?**

It takes time, especially if you've been practicing the limiting MindStory for a long time. To reinforce the empowering MindStory you can do a new AVARA Model often on the same area of life.

12. **What is the difference between the VISION part of the AVARA Model and the REPROGRAM part?**

In the limiting column, the VISION is a way your life might turn out ONE YEAR from now, if you keep living from this limiting MindStory. For example, "I will have a mediocre business at best". In the empowering column, the VISION is a way your life might turn out ONE YEAR from now, if you choose to live from this empowering MindStory. For example, "I will have created a profitable business". Whereas, REPROGRAM is a moment in the recent past that triggered this issue (in the limiting MindStory column). Then, it's a possible moment in time that's likely to happen in the near future, that's more empowering (in the right hand column).

Making it Stick

If you made it this far, that tells us something about you. Our guess is that you care about doing your best, and you want to make sure these ideas don't just stay as ideas. In fact, many people ask us, how can I make an empowering MindStory stick? Sometimes you can just do the AVARA Model once, or apply one of the other tools in this book, and it will stick. However, if you notice the same issue coming up over and over again, chances are you've been reinforcing a complicated MindStory for decades. Not only that but we all have a multitude of limiting MindStories that have been there causing havoc for decades.

Don't underestimate the power of the old, entrenched MindStories. Even people who've done years of personal growth, who are coaches themselves and experts on this topic, including both of us...still get caught out. It's really important to be honest with yourself, and to not let your ego convince you that you've transcended all this. That's one of the biggest traps. High achievers commit to clearing out and resetting their mind daily. Just like brushing your teeth. Otherwise, the limiting MindStories will continue to run your life.

Here are several suggestions:

1. **Do the AVARA Model daily:** In fact do it every time a negative feeling or thought takes over. Be warned that sometimes you are unaware this is happening. Much of it is happening at a subconscious level. Look for symptoms such as physical tension, negative results in your life, or wanting to distract yourself with work, social media, busyness, food or other addictions.

2. Check out more **Free Resources** at MindStory Academy here: https://MindstoryAcademy.com/#free. There you'll find self-assessments, free webinars, 5-day trials of our popular courses, and more.

3. **Join M.I.C . – The MindStory Inner Circle**
https://MindStoryAcademy.com/Join/
This is our coaching membership program designed to:
   - keep your head in the game as a business owner and leader in your field
   - take all this material and truly master it
   - get on-going inspiration and accountability to move forward
   - receive group and 1-to-1 help to customize all this just for you
   - be part of a like-minded, supportive community of people
   - get access to many more tools to break yourself free
   - get strategies to build your business quickly and to communicate with power, purpose and passion

MINDSTORY COACHING CERTIFICATION PROGRAM

https://MindStoryAcademy.com/Certification/

Do you want to be trained as a top-notch performance coach? You get to:

- go to a whole other level of mastery with these skills by teaching them to others
- be part of a dynamic, like-minded community of coaches supporting each other to be their best
- get training as a MindStory Performance Coach so you can earn excellent income while also making a huge difference for others

You can join the Entrepreneurial Track and add the MindStory tools to your coaching business. Or, you can join the For Hire Track and work for us or another company as a coach.

About the Authors

Carla Rieger is the author of 6 books and more than 10 online learning programs. She's been the CEO of The Artistry of Change Coaching & Training Inc. since 2014, and a speaker, trainer and coach for over 23 years. As a marketing, mindset and communication skills expert, she's helped thousands of people all over the world lead more fulfilling and successful lives through her performance enhancement tools. In addition, she has spoken to over 1500 groups on four continents, including a TEDx talk. She is also the host of the MindStory SPEAKER Podcast.

For over 20 years, Dave O'Connor has been a keynote speaker and highly regarded international performance coach to conscious business owners, entrepreneurs, visionary leaders, coaches and consultants. Dave specializes in engaging keynote speeches and offers live and online trainings in the areas of mindset, leadership, communication, storytelling, and influence skills. Dave is also the co-founder of MindStory Academy with his partner Carla Rieger, helping mission driven business owners to break free from negative patterns and limiting stories, so they can fulfil their greatest life's potential. Dave has a background that includes Humanistic Neuro-Linguistic Psychology, Performance Mindset Conditioning and the Psychology of Attention. He is also the host of the MindStory COACH podcast.

Notes

Lightning Source UK Ltd.
Milton Keynes UK
UKHW022020260919
350504UK00008B/289/P